The Feminine Mistake

Cal Samra

NASH PUBLISHING

Los Angeles

Library of Congress Catalog Card Number: 73-167514
Standard Book Number: 8402-1209-7

Published by Nash Publishing in cooperation with
The Society for the Emancipation of the American Male
P. O. Box 211, Ann Arbor, Michigan 48104

Published simultaneously in the United States and
Canada by Nash Publishing, 9255 Sunset Boulevard,
Los Angeles, California 90069.

Printed in the United States of America

First printing

To Kathleen

A good wife, a good mother, and a good woman

Would there were more like her,
methinks there would be
fewer wars, riots, and madhouses

THE LOCKHORNS

"ABOUT THIS NEW APPLICANT.....IF HE
SAYS HE'S HAPPILY MARRIED
HE MAY LIE ABOUT OTHER THINGS, TOO."

World Without End

Those with a childish leader perish; those with a female leader perish.
>—Hindu proverb, circa 950 B.C., expressing
>alarm at the anarchy of India

As for my people, children are their oppressors, and women rule over them.
>—Isaiah, circa 780 B.C., alarmed at
>the fall of Israel

Children are the rulers of their parents, and women find joy in men's clothing.
>—Aristotle, circa 300 B.C., alarmed at
>the civil strife in Greece

And the children shall rise up against their parents, and cause them to be put to death . . . And a man's foes shall be they of his own household.
>—Jesus Christ,
>prophesying the fall of Israel

What? Shall Allah have daughters and not sons?
>—The Prophet Mohammed, circa 620 A.D.,
>alarmed at the warfare between the Arabian
>tribes worshipping goddesses

American women began to lose control of their children when they ceased to submit to the control of their husbands.
>—C. Northcote Parkinson, 1968 A.D.,
>alarmed by the riots and demonstrations he
>found while on a visit to America

Fighting and love belong together.
>—Adolf Hitler

When religious feeling wanes in a society, it means that woman's power is waxing.
>—Tolstoy

Contents

Acknowledgments

For their generous assistance in producing this book, I wish to thank the many psychiatrists, psychologists, clergymen, marriage counselors, social workers, doctors, and lawyers who contributed so much of their time and thought, but who preferred to remain anonymous lest their wives find them out. My gratitude, too, to the many reporters who inquired about SEAM, and who passed on items of interest; to Dr. Walter C. Alvarez for his wise counsel and encouragement; to Glenn D. Kittler of *Coronet* for his sympathetic ear; to Phon E. Hudkins of the U.S. Department of Labor for the statistics regarding male and female employment; to E. N. Kurtz, John Brinson, and the He-Man's Message Association for their undying allegiance to what many regard as a lost cause; to Hugh E. Geyer of Morristown, New Jersey, a vice-president of an international corporation, for his thoughts on "the Great American Put-Down"; and to psychologist Paul Popenoe, president of the American Institute of Family Relations, Los Angeles, for his statistics.

I also wish to thank the members and correspondents of the Society for the Emancipation of the American Male for their contributions, news clippings, and thoughtful letters; and Gunther Stuhlmann, Mavis McIntosh, Jim Langford, and Professor Fred S. Siebert for their editorial advice.

Special thanks to William P. Hoest and King Features Syndicate for their permission to reprint The Lockhorns panels, a delightful new cartoon strip that is now appearing in many newspapers around the country. (Mr. Hoest tells us that The Lockhorns strip is "gaining in popularity, proving, I think, that the American Male refuses to lie down and take it any longer." He adds that he believes "there does exist a small minority of males who have never relinquished their position of head of the household. May their numbers increase. And long live the Society!")

For the other illustrations appearing in this volume, my thanks to artist Bill Robinson and Doris Blake of *The New York Daily News* for their permission to reprint Mr. Robinson's illustration; to artist Helge W. Sahlin and Richard W. O'Donnell of *The Boston Globe* for their permission to reprint Miss Sahlin's illustration; to artist Jon Buechel and Jennifer Jarratt of *The Detroit Free Press* for their permission to reprint Mr. Buechel's illustration; and to Jim Berry and the Newspaper Enterprise Association for permission to reprint the panel from Berry's World.

Special thanks, too, to Professor Moshe Kapliwatsky, the eminent historian, anthropologist, and archeologist, for the report on that ancient patriarchal paradise, Tabboola, which is made public in this volume for the first time.

Finally, my thanks to my wife, Kathleen, for her encouragement, for her excellent typing skills, and for that increasingly rare human virtue: her loyalty.

CAL SAMRA

Introduction:
Samra's Complaint

It is in the nature of things that newspapers have women's sections, but not men's sections. There is, perhaps, no master more oppressive than a mistress; and the neo-feminists, the Women's Liberationists, and their male collaborators have come near to excluding all points of view save their own. Feminist propaganda has become so shrill and pervasive in recent years, with no voices being raised to rebut it, that we felt compelled to publish this modest, lonely little book in the hope that the public and students would have at least *one* source book stating those facts and notions which the feminists would prefer to ignore.

This book, perhaps the first true masculinist tract since the Koran, is a product of nearly seven years of diligent and sustained research, during which I interviewed and corresponded with hundreds of persons, some of whom were afraid to talk, but none of whom were reluctant to talk. A common complaint of my correspondents and those who wrote letters to the Society for the Emancipation of the American Male, of which I am one of the founders, was that they had submitted their manuscripts to various publishers and news media, but no one ever bothered to publish them. So this book has got to be some kind of first.

In point of fact, there are only a handful of feminist organizations in the United States, including the Women's Liberation Movement and the National Organization for Women. In contrast, there are more than *fifty* masculinist, men's rights, and divorce reform organizations. (A list of them may be found at the end of this book.) It is perhaps a measure of the madness of our times that the activities of the masculinist organizations are rarely, if ever, reported. Hardly anyone knows they exist. But then what else can one expect in a nation whose rose societies give annual awards for the roses judged to be the queen of the show, the princess of the show, and the prince of the show—but have nothing for the king.

Perhaps it might not be altogether clear to some readers why a layman who served as executive director of a psychiatric research organization should be regarded as qualified to write a book about women. But for centuries poets, philosophers, and wise men have insisted that they perceived a relationship between madness and women. And during my years with the psychiatric organization I found no evidence that they were wrong.

It was while I was working for the organization that I came into contact with numerous psychiatrists, psychologists, marriage counselors, doctors, and clergymen who were concerned about the decline and emasculation of the American male (including themselves), the dominance of American women, and the breakdown of the American family. One often sensed that the professionals, when they went home—if they went home—at the end of a hard day, shared precisely the same problems with their patients, but the professionals merely had a higher pain threshold. I often wondered why most of the men I knew on the board of directors of one mental health organization either worked at their offices sixteen hours a day and weekends, or traveled to far-off places continuously, or both. They were rarely home.

Studying the histories of both the psychiatric movement and the feminist movement in America, I discovered a rather curious parallel in their growth during the past hundred years. I called this interesting fact to the attention of several of my psychiatrist friends whose opinions I greatly esteemed. They were, of course, amused, and promptly went back to their medical and molecular models.

In the eighteen-seventies, after the Civil War, when the women's emancipation movement first began gaining partisans in America, there were only a handful of medical men—then called "alienists"—who specialized in treating diseases of the mind; and for the most part these men worked as administrators only, staying within the confines of lunatic asylums. It was only when the feminist movement blossomed and gained momentum in the latter part of the nineteenth century that the "alienists" came out of their asylums, called themselves psychiatrists, and began to treat an expanding market of patients on the outside.

By the time women had won their voting rights, economic power, and virtual equality on all levels in the nineteen-sixties, a new and huge industry had grown up employing thousands of psychiatrists, psychologists, marriage counselors, social workers, doctors, clergymen, and other professionals, who were valiantly and frantically occupied in trying to contain a massive epidemic of psychiatric disorders, alcoholism, drug addiction, divorce, desertions, identity crises, homosexuality, lesbianism, impotence, heart attacks, premature deaths, widowing, wife-murdering, suicide, juvenile delinquency, violence, and riots.

Today, our madhouses are filled with people who believe in the equality of men and women, and we can't build hospitals fast enough and big enough to accommodate them all. Women are in the forefront of the mental health movement. About 11 percent of American psychiatrists are women, and their numbers grow each year. At the time of this writing the executive director of the National Council on Alcoholism was a woman; the president of the National Association for Mental Health was a woman; the president of the National Society for Autistic Children was a woman. Women by far made up the mass of the membership of the organization I worked for, as they do of all mental health organizations, searching for a cure for the madness of which they themselves, perhaps, are the principal cause.

Something had to be done, and in the summer of 1969 a group of us in Ann Arbor formed the Society for the Emancipation of the American Male (SEAM). The aims of the new Society, we announced in a news release to the press, were: to restore the American patriarchy, preserve the family, return the male to his rightful place at the head of the family, and free him from discriminatory divorce, alimony, and custody laws.

We were unprepared for the staggering response. Every major newspaper and wire service in the country carried lengthy articles on the Society—with perhaps the notable exception of Mary Baker Eddy's *Christian Science Monitor*.

Articles on SEAM appeared as far away as Okinawa and Saudi Arabia. Some newspapers carried the story on their front page; but, not insignificantly, in the majority of the cases it wound up in the women's section. SEAM's news release, we were told, produced gales of laughter in many city rooms; but overall, the press was divided as to whether to treat the story lightly or seriously. (See press notices on pages 219-248.)

The publicity resulted in numerous telegrams, telephone calls, radio and television invitations, and thousands of letters and requests for membership in both the Society and its Ladies Auxiliary. A surprising number of women begged us to allow them to join our Ladies Auxiliary. It was clear that we had touched a sensitive nerve in the American body politic.

Not long after the formation of the Society, we received an invitation from a major university's historical manuscripts library to donate SEAM's letters and records to the library, as they "will be of certain interest to historians and sociologists in the years to come."

Following this invitation, we set to work making an analysis of the thousands of letters the Society had received. We found that:

98 percent of the letter writers expressed unqualified and enthusiastic support of SEAM's aims.

Fully 20 percent of the letter writers were women, and most were all for SEAM.

Most of the letter writers complained about America's divorce and child-custody laws, which they regarded as being grossly unfair to the male.

Perhaps most significantly, fully 39 percent of the letter

7

writers carried names which suggest they are probably immigrants or the children of immigrants.

The letter writers broke down as follows by national origin:

Persons of Italian origin represented the largest number of letter writers (all approving), reaching 15 percent of the total.
The Irish were a close second, with 12 percent.
Poles, Greeks, Armenians, Germans, Eastern Europeans, South Americans, Canadians, and Lebanese were also well represented. (*The Lebanese-American Journal*, published in New York, carried an article about one of the founders of SEAM under the headline: "You Might Have Known He'd Be Lebanese.")

We speculated that the high percentage of Italian and other foreign names among letter writers might arise because these persons have recently come from countries where they have savored the benefits of patriarchy. And the inevitable outcries of indignation upon their first encounter with the American matriarchy (as when one reacts to putting one's hand over a burning candle) is merely a measure of their special sensitivity to the contrasts in the two styles of living. The foreigners have not yet resigned themselves to their new fate, and so might be expected to protest more.

Also, perhaps significantly, a substantial number of letter writers identified themselves as servicemen serving overseas, and therefore presumably in a position to compare the benefits of living in a patriarchy with those in a matriarchy, such as they are.

But I am ahead of myself.

The question of what constitutes the right relationship between men and women has occupied philosophers and writers for centuries, and often their lives have depended upon how they answered it. It is the mother (or rather the father) of most humor as well as most tragedy, and so the reader is likely to find this book by turns hilarious and calamitous.

CAL SAMRA

The
Feminine
Mistake

The Problem That Has a Name, and a Statistical View of the American Matriarchy

Listen carefully, O Beloved One, for I come to reveal to you what the Almighty, Blessed Be His Name, has given only to his Chosen Ones. And for receiving it and declaring it publicly, these men suffered all manner of persecution at the hands of the Infidels, may their souls burn in Everlasting Fire! One's head, that of John the Baptist, was presented on a platter to Salome. Another was crucified. A third, the one they called Paul, the windy one, was jailed many times. Others were stoned to death.

Listen, for I speak of the Mysteries of the Universe. It is written in the Book that a woman has the power to take a man either to heaven or to hell. And this is so, as it was then and shall be unto the end of Time. For while I was setting down these words upon these sacred pages, a number of events conspired to transpire which, God be praised, testify

*to the Infinite Wisdom of the Holy Scriptures. God is indeed
great, and shall send forth his curses upon those who deny his
Name. Woe unto Them! For shall God have daughters and
not sons? Only dogs sit at the feet of women. Listen!*

In Boston, Edgar A. Collis testified in court that his wife
beat him with an angle iron while his son bashed him with a
snow shovel and his daughter struck him with a broom. The
state supreme court dismissed Collis' suit for divorce, ruling
that he had not proved he had suffered cruel and abusive
treatment. Collis had appealed the decision of a probate
court judge who said the episode was "a typical husband-
and-wife brawl."

In New York, after she was released as a suspect in a
bombing, accosted in jail by lesbians, and swindled by a
woman posing as a federal agent, Mrs. Mary Almeida de
Ortiz, an Ecuadorian visitor, commented: "You call my
country underdeveloped! Compared to this, I live in the Holy
Land."

Jackie Gleason, Groucho Marx, Dick Smothers, and Betty
Friedan, the author of *The Feminine Mystique*, were divorced from their mates. (Groucho's third wife sued and won
a $1 million settlement because she was insulted when her
husband complained about her cooking.) Cass Elliott was
awarded a divorce from her songwriter husband, James
Hendricks, after she testified he became jealous "as I became
more famous," and "used to yell and scream and throw tan-
trums." Andy Williams, Franklin D. Roosevelt, Jr., Steven
Rockefeller, and former New York Mayor Robert F. Wagner
separated from their wives. Lana Turner married for the
seventh time, and Roswell Gilpatric for the fourth. A California couple obtained their fifth divorce—from each other—
in twenty years.

In Chicago, Dr. Edward Goldfarb, a psychiatrist, was sued for divorce by his wife, Dr. June Goldfarb, also a psychiatrist. The judge ordered the couple to see a psychiatrist in a reconciliation attempt.

The wife of pro football's premier quarterback Johnny Unitas filed for divorce, charging adultery. And the day after they celebrated their seventh wedding anniversary, Jim Wynn, Houston Astros outfielder, was stabbed by his wife during an argument.

In Santa Ana, California, the wife of President Nixon's longtime political adviser, Murray Chotiner, filed for divorce. Chotiner told the court that before he was married five years ago, he had $48,000 in bank accounts. "After the marriage," he said, "I had to borrow money to pay household expenses." He is now deeply in debt.

In New York, Johnny Carson's actress wife sued for divorce, asking for $7,000 a week in alimony. Arthur Schlesinger, Jr., and Dr. Albert E. Sabin separated from their wives. Former Arkansas Governor Winthrop Rockefeller announced that he and his wife have separated and will be divorced. It was the fourth marriage for the former Jeannette Edris, one of the leading lights in the National Association for Mental Health.

In Juarez, Diana Hartford, a former model, obtained a divorce from Huntington Hartford, millionaire A & P supermarket heir, on grounds of incompatability and immediately announced she would celebrate with a "glorious jaunt to Europe." Actress Patty Duke was divorced March 3, 1970, from her first husband, married for the second time June 23, saying "we have no particular plans but to stay together forever," and divorced her second husband July 22.

Explaining that "an increasing number of women are single, divorced or widowed," Isabella Taves, a widow and former *Look* magazine reporter, began writing a new column called "Women Alone," telling women how to cope with the problems of living without men. In her own very popular column, Abigail Van Buren advised still another wife to send still another husband to a psychiatrist for an examination, an increasingly stock answer from dear Abby.

In Los Angeles, Superior Court Judge Lloyd S. Davis told a court that he was temporarily deranged when he stabbed his wife with a knife. His wife agreed. Dame Judith Anderson announced she would tour the country playing Hamlet, Dr. Cynthia Wedel was elected the first woman president of the National Council of Churches, President Nixon nominated two women to be the Army's first women generals, and a woman finally broke the men-only barrier of the FBI's Ten Most Wanted List.

In Canton, Georgia, a man walked quietly into a special Mother's Day service at a Baptist church and shot his wife. And in Detroit, a twenty-one-year-old man was shotgunned to death by his bride of five hours. James Roosevelt was stabbed in the back by his third wife; the daughter of Gene Tunney was committed to a mental hospital after she bludgeoned her husband to death on an Easter Sunday; and millionaire William E. Thoresen III was shot to death during a quarrel with his wife, who had earlier filed for divorce.

In Enid, Oklahoma, the father-in-law of Senator Birch Bayh was reported by police to have shot and killed his wife and then turned the gun on himself after a quarrel. The murder-suicide occurred, ironically, while the senator, who is chairman of the Constitutional Rights Subcommittee, was holding a hearing in Washington on women's rights. The sympathetic senator told a group of feminists, "You must stimulate national concern and prick the national conscience if we are to succeed." Not a single male showed up at the hearing.

THE LOCKHORNS

"THE WAY I HEARD IT, HE SHOT HIS WIFE DURING A PERIOD OF TEMPORARY SANITY."

In Norwalk, Connecticut, a twenty-seven-year-old father of three shot himself to death during an argument with his wife. In Napa, California, Charles Bray, enraged by a divorce suit filed by his wife, went berserk, killed six of his seven children, set his house on fire, and killed himself. In Oakland, California, Leo Gorcey, who as leader of Hollywood's "Dead End Kids" had survived numerous street fights, died at the youthful age of fifty-two after five turbulent marriages. A top official of a major college killed himself because of marital difficulties.

In New York City, a city policewoman fatally shot her husband, a police sergeant; while in Ypsilanti, Michigan, an ex-sheriff's deputy shot his wife in the head in a telephone booth after the final argument in a tempestuous marriage.

Also in Ypsilanti, Ronald B. Lewis, twenty-two, was stabbed to death by a sixteen-year-old girl following a quarrel, less than a year after his wife had been stabbed to death by another juvenile girl. Ypsilanti State Hospital, meantime, announced that it was opening its first integrated male-female ward—one of many madhouses which, along with fraternities, schools, and bars, decided to go coed.

THE LOCKHORNS

"I STOOD UP TO APPLAUD HIS ACTING ABILITY·····NOT BECAUSE HE WAS STRANGLING HIS WIFE."

In Washington, Jules L. Pierce was arrested after he interrupted a speech by Representative Edith Green appealing for more women in the antipoverty program. "That woman's all wet," Pierce had shouted from the galleries. "Women have too much say in this country already." He was spirited away in handcuffs.

In Philadelphia, William R. Welch observed his 107th birthday with this formula for longevity: "I never got married."

In Lamar, South Carolina, howling whites—many of them

women—battered and overturned school buses bringing black students to a formerly all-white school. In New York, the FBI pressed a hunt for Kathy Boudin, a leader of the Students for a Democratic Society, in the investigation of a bomb factory explosion on West 11th Street. In Chicago, Miss Boudin was wanted by police on a charge of wielding a club against two policemen the day of the Chicago conspiracy trial. She had earlier been arrested on charges of "aggravated battery" after striking a policeman during a demonstration in Grant Park. Also arrested was Cathy Wilkerson, described as "a violent Quaker" and a member of the Weatherman's "Women's Militia," on a charge of assaulting a policeman with a four-foot club.

A federal grand jury subsequently indicted thirteen members of the Weathermen—*seven of them women*, including Kathy Boudin and Cathy Wilkerson—charging them with conspiracy to commit bombings in New York, Chicago, and Berkeley. They were said to have planned to build a nationwide revolutionary network to bomb police, business, and educational buildings throughout the country and "to kill and injure persons therein."

In Vietnam, Army officials began to report that servicewomen were complaining that they were not being sent into combat. And in Ann Arbor, Mrs. Harriet Powers, a housewife and former teacher, shook her head in bewilderment during a campaign for election to the board of education. "The seventh and eighth grades have always been turbulent times, and most boys fight at this age," she said in reply to a question from a parent concerned about the rising incidence of drug addiction, vandalism, and violence in the public schools. "What bothers me now," Mrs. Powers added, "is the girls are beginning to fight." The Ann Arbor school board had earlier released a report on the disturbances indicating that five of seven victims of physical assaults were girls, and seven of eight victims of verbal intimidations also were girls.

Indeed, the level of violence in the once peaceful town of Ann Arbor appeared to increase almost in direct proportion to the number of coeds who enrolled at its great university. In 1953 there were 10,655 coeds enrolled at the University of Michigan; by 1968 there were 14,973, or almost 39.4 percent of the total enrollment. By the end of the sixties, idyllic Ann Arbor was racked by student riots, confrontations, bomb-throwings, muggings, assaults, and the community was terrorized by a series of coed slayings. Nine college coeds were found slain over a period of two years, and all three of the young men arrested and charged with the murders, police found, came from broken homes and never knew their fathers. The women of Ann Arbor became increasingly afraid to walk the streets alone, day or night.

Ann Arbor's city council responded to this chaos, in part, by adopting a revised disorderly conduct code. The code starts off as follows under the subtitle "Acts Prohibited": "Masculine pronouns in this section shall be construed to include both male and female persons . . ."

"America's families are in trouble—trouble so deep and pervasive as to threaten the future of our nation," declared a recent report to the White House Conference on Children. And *Time* magazine, in a windy report in which its researchers interviewed and quoted seemingly every professional person except (curiously) clergymen, agreed that the future of the American family is decidedly uncertain. *Time*, whose affections in recent years have shifted from Dr. Jung to Dr. Freud and Dr. Laing, quoted at length psychologist David Cooper, author of *The Death of the Family*, who believes that "the bourgeois nuclear family" is "a fur-lined bear trap."

With our entire society plunging into an age of chaos and darkness which may rival medieval times, perhaps the time has come to ask the unforgivable:

Why is it that our society produces so many women-haters who appear in one form or another?

Why is it that the fiercest faces you find seem to be on the feminists and the homosexuals?

Why are women increasingly afraid to walk the streets alone, day or night?

Why so much senseless violence?

Could it be because so many women are shunning the tender, loving, supportive, feminine role of wife and mother that all sane and civilized societies have cherished through the centuries? Could it be because the homes of our men are no longer sanctuaries, but battlegrounds, and all this family turmoil tends to spill over into our streets and into our schools? Surely it couldn't be so simple.

But the facts are clear and simple, and together they constitute what some will presume, with good reason, to be an indictment of the feminist movement. To go straight to the mark, without dallying—this is what we have come to after a century of feminism:

Every year in America, a half-million (or one out of four) marriages end in divorce. Two of four marriages suffer from "emotional divorce," as one psychiatrist calls it—or in other words, the couples would gladly murder one another if the law would permit it. Eight million American fathers have deserted their families and no longer support them. One in eight (or about nine million) marriageable American men is a bachelor.

There are, conservatively, ten million homosexuals in America. And psychiatrists have become alarmed by the spread of homosexuality. Doctors have observed that many homosexuals started out by putting women on pedestals and ended by becoming confirmed women haters. Some students of the feminist movement have noted its curious relationship to the homosexual movement. The French homosexual Jean Genet has become the favorite author of the Women's Liberationists. On one campus, members of the Gay Liberation League, picketing for permission to hold a dance, were joined by neo-feminists carrying signs proclaiming, "Women's Liberation Supports Gay Liberation."

There are also up to 78.6 million masturbators in America and 27.3 million adulterers, at a time when, *Time* magazine informs us, "adultery has become a lighthearted and guilt-free pastime." Additionally, there are seven million alcoholics and twenty million mentally ill persons.

There are nine million widows in the United States. The American widow touring Europe has become a familiar sight, and the average life-span of the male shrinks with each passing decade. The American male ranks thirty-first in terms of the average remaining lifetime from the age of ten, according to the National Advisory Committee on Manpower.

There are six million unemployed men in America at a time when a third of the working force is made up of women.

There are four million male moonlighters.

There is a plague of fatherless, homeless, and emotionally disturbed children, runaways, and juvenile delinquents.

Three-fifths of all psychiatric patients are male, many of them suffering from sexual impotence, identity crises, anxiety, depression. Three of every four suicides are male.

Fully half of all traffic fatalities are caused by drunk drivers, and according to a recent study by a University of

Michigan psychiatrist, 20 percent of a group of drunk drivers responsible for fatal accidents had been acutely upset and had had violent quarrels with women—wives, girl friends, barmaids, and female drinking companions—immediately preceding the fatal accident.

THE LOCKHORNS

"NO, I DIDN'T GROWL AT YOU....THAT WAS THE GARBAGE DISPOSAL."

One out of every ten homicides has something to do with romantic passions or jealousy, according to FBI statistics.

Ninety percent of our prison population has come from broken homes.

In the America of the sixties there were not a few men who came to the conclusion that it was easier to be a woman than a man in our society. This was a time when sex-change operations, through surgery and treatment with the hormone estrogen, became popular. A psychiatrist reported that three to four males for every female want to switch sexes. And when Marie Anderson, women's editor of *The Miami Herald*, learned of the formation of SEAM, she sent us a news clipping noting this fact, with the comment, "You'd better stick with being males, emancipated or otherwise, and fight the good fight, rather than joining us if you can't lick us."

One does not get the full import of these figures until one adds them all up, as shown in Figure 1.

We see, therefore, that approximately 306,180,000 persons in the United States have been, in one way or another, victimized by a system which punishes both the guilty and the innocent. Let us not allow the fact that the population of the United States is somewhat less than our total figure to distract us from the awesome import of these statistics. Our statistics were checked and double-checked with numerous private and public institutions which will vouchsafe for their accuracy. The fact that our total statistics are somewhat larger than the population of the United States may simply be attributed to the fact that a person may fit into more than one category, and thus be recorded several times. Thus the same man may be a bachelor, get married, be divorced, become a homosexual, take to drink, have a sex-switch operation, kill his ex-wife, participate in a street riot, run somebody down in his car after a quarrel with a barmaid, and finally, die of a heart attack. Not a really uncommon sequence of events in this day and age.

For the past several years our government officials and public leaders have commissioned numerous studies to find out why there is so much violence in America. I submit that the search is no longer necessary since the foregoing statistics, when seen as they are here in combination for the first time, fully explain the reasons why. It would take a feat of remarkable endurance for a man to live in such a society for long without becoming unbalanced or violent sooner or later—and more likely sooner.

FIGURE 1

A Statistical View of the American Matriarchy

30 million divorcés and divorcées
60 million "emotional" divorcés and divorcées
8 million males who have deserted their families
10 million homosexuals
.03 million transsexuals
9 million bachelors
78.6 million masturbators
27.3 million adulterers and adulteresses
20 million mentally ill persons (60% of them male)
7 million alcoholics
1 million heart attacks caused by the normal strains
   of family life
9 million widows
6 million unemployed men displaced by women
4 million male moonlighters who'd rather not come home
.2 million male suicides and attempted suicides
.75 million juvenile delinquents and runaways
1 million convicts and criminals who have come from
   broken homes
.3 million traffic fatalities caused by drunk drivers,
   following violent quarrels with wives, girl friends
   and barmaids
.1 million homicides related to romantic passion and
   jealousy
11 million sexually impotent men
22.4 million sexually frigid women
.2 million drug addicts
.3 million rioters

_____

Total: 306.18 million

THE LOCKHORNS

"OUR ANNIVERSARY AND PEARL HARBOR
ARE TWO DATES I NEVER FORGET!"

Samra's Law
and Ancient Tabboola

Time and again in the feminist century, the world was brought to the brink of annihilation by an assortment of militarists, tyrants, and revolutionaries, many of whom were confirmed women haters. Campuses were burned by rampaging students, many of whom—as psychiatrist Dr. A. M. Nicholi II of the Harvard Medical School recently reported— came from broken homes or boarding houses and never knew their busy or absent fathers and never learned how to accept male authority gracefully. They had become so accustomed to taking orders all their lives from women—their mothers, female teachers, girl friends, and wives—that an order from a man completely unnerved them. And they went berserk.

"American women," observed visiting Englishman C. Northcote Parkinson, "began to lose control of their children when they ceased to submit to the control of their hubands."

And indeed, nobody was listening to father. A study by the New Jersey YMCA found that most teenagers rated their fathers as poor advisers, and they took their problems to their mothers first. ("Dear Torn: I don't blame Gloria for not wanting her Dad to chauffer her and her date to the prom. Better tell Dad that if Gloria had had the proper upbringing, he wouldn't have to worry about her behavior at age 16. And if he insists on chaperoning her much longer, not to be surprised if Gloria decides to move out of the house at the earliest moment. Abby.")

THE LOCKHORNS

"SUPPOSE I PUT DOWN UNDECIDED!"

The Society for the Emancipation of the American Male has just completed an exhaustive, in-depth study of the lives and biographies of the foremost tyrants, revolutionaries, assassins, and troublemakers of the past century. We discovered that the great majority of them were confirmed women haters. Many of them had suffered through turbulent marriages and were subsequently divorced. In the backgrounds of these violent men—and women—one almost always found a failure to establish a tender, loving, and enduring relationship with a member of the opposite sex. (We shall discuss these violent men in a later chapter.)

With the assistance of a number of eminent historians, scholars, sociologists, psychiatrists, and criminologists, the Society also made a comprehensive study of the world's major civilizations, following them through the patriarchal and matriarchal stages of their development. The study was initially funded by the National Institute of Madness, but I regret to say that funds were cut back as soon as it became clear what the thrust of the conclusions was going to be. I also regret to say that great efforts were made to suppress this report by certain prominent individuals, both in private and public life, whom I would prefer not to identify at this time.

The results of our interdisciplinary scholarship led to the discovery of a new principle at work in the history of nations, which until now only a few avatars have perceived. And those who perceived it were to suffer greatly for declaring it publicly.

Samra's Law

At the risk of similar persecution, I herewith advance my proposition, which I will call, for no other reason than to have my name immortalized, Samra's Law, and that is:

All great civilizations have begun and flowered as patriarchies and have grown progressively madder, more warlike, more violent, and more ungovernable as they have declined into matriarchies.

Or, in other words:

Nations grow mad in direct proportion to the degree of freedom they allow their women.

Or, restated:

The wilder the women, the crazier the country.

An algebraic equation can clearly depict these relationships, and we used alphabetical notations in the formula as follows:

MF = madness factor
P = the number of psychiatrists in any society
f = the number of voting feminists
a = the number of adulteresses
w = the number of widows
$\sqrt{x}$ = the square root of the number of homosexuals
m = the number of committed madmen
d = the number of drunks
c = the number of convicts
s = the number of suicides

Reduced to its simplest algebraic formula, Samra's Law, Principle, and Complaint may be seen in Figure 2.

FIGURE 2

$$MF = \frac{P}{f^2} = 3a + w - \sqrt{x} + m^2 + d + c + s \; \mathsf{X} \; \frac{f}{10}$$

Thus MF (madness factor) in any society may be determined by dividing the number of psychiatrists in that society by the number of voting feminists squared, which in turn is precisely equal to the sum of the number of adulteresses taken three times plus the number of widows minus the square root of the number of homosexuals plus the number of committed madmen squared and the sum of the drunks, convicts, and suicides, multiplied by the number of voting feminists divided by ten.

In making a comparative study of the madness factors of various civilizations, past and present, I was fortunate to have the generous assistance of Professor Moshe Kapliwatsky, the eminent historian, anthropologist, and archeologist who, I might add, was raised in a Hasidic community and who shares many of SEAM's views. "It is better," says Professor Kapliwatsky, quoting, I think, Proverbs 21:19, "to dwell in the wilderness than with a contentious and angry woman." Without the scholarship and enthusiasm of Professor Kapliwatsky, this volume would not have been possible.

The civilization with the lowest madness factor, we discovered, existed about forty-five hundred years before the birth of Christ and survived into the fourth century A.D. This small nation, about which little was known until Professor Kapliwatsky returned from his expedition in the early sixties, was called Tabboola. It was nestled in a rich and fertile valley, surrounded by towering, snow-capped mountains, in what is now Southern Russia but which used to be the northernmost borders of Persia and Armenia.

The people of Tabboola were a gentle, good-natured, fun-loving, and unwarlike people, and indeed for four thousand years the records show that, until late in their history, they never engaged in a war with their neighbors, nor suffered through a civil war or a revolution. Little is left of this ancient civilization except a few scrolls evidently written by the first of its great rulers, the wise old King Tut-a-Tut-Tut.

According to Professor Kapliwatsky, who after some initial

31

difficulty mastered the strange language of the Tabboolans, King Tut-a-Tut-Tut set the pattern for his successors and subjects for many centuries to come, with a series of royal proclamations. Each Tabboolan man was declared unequivocally to be the lord and master of his home and supported in this claim by the law of the realm and the power of the crown. The word of each man, to his wife and to his children, was to be honored and obeyed as if it had proceeded from the very lips of the sovereign himself. And to dispute that word was to dispute the king.

Women as well as children were to be beaten and sequestered if they quarreled with the head of the household or misbehaved. Every wife in the nation was ordered by royal decree to be a good wife to her husband and to serve him cheerfully and faithfully. Women could not hold public office, nor conduct business in the marketplace, own property, attend school, or go to church. They could not sue for divorce or for alimony. The privilege of divorce was reserved solely for the man if his wife repeatedly neglected her duties as a wife and failed to please him. But woe to the woman whose husband divorced her; for not only did the court give the custody of the children to the father, but she also became a social outcast. No honorable and self-esteeming Tabboolan man would have anything to do with her afterwards. And the chances were good that even her own friends and family would disown her.

"You see," said Professor Kapliwatsky gleefully, unable to conceal his joy at his discovery of such a well-ordered world, "the Tabboolan women were *forced* to be good wives and mothers. They were simply given no other alternatives."

The Tabboolan men, according to Professor Kapliwatsky, were perhaps the longest-lived men in the history of civilization. They were known for their endurance and good health, and rare was the male who did not attain the age of 125. The widow of any man who died before reaching the age of eighty-five was exiled from the kingdom. Legend has it that King Tut-a-Tut-Tut himself lived to 175 and his wife to 135. Professor Kapliwatsky said he could find no evidence of a geriatric service in the sparse records of the civilization. It appears, however, that heart attacks were practically unheard of and widows were rare sights to behold.

The men, unencumbered by marital and family conflicts and problems, were freed to pursue the development of their minds and their bodies. They excelled in sports, in the arts, in the sciences, and in philosophy, reports Professor Kapliwatsky. Art and poetry and music flourished, but this art extolled the beauty of the human body and spirit. Architecturally, the temples of Tabboola surpassed the Greek and the Roman in grace, style, and beauty. Their music was unrivaled and had a special quality of gaiety about it. And their poetry, romantic by our standards, sang of the loveliness and charm of the women of Tabboola.

"In one of those curious ironies of history," explains Professor Kapliwatsky, "King Tut-a-Tut-Tut, by humbling the women of Tabboola, exalted them, and all the men of the kingdom sang their praises, and the women walked the streets of the kingdom's cities at night without fear. The Tabboolans were a happy people. Their children were well mannered, obedient, and courteous. They knew nothing of alcoholism, homosexuality, juvenile delinquency. As far as can be determined, there is no evidence that they had either mental institutions or prisons. A great civilization!"

The Tabboolan civilization, for reasons which are not entirely clear, vanished about 374 A.D. and left few traces.

But according to certain artifacts found by Professor Kapliwatsky at the site of his excavations, it appears that the decline began when one of King Tut-a-Tut-Tut's princely descendants found himself with no male heirs to the crown. When the last of the Tabboolan kings died, one of his daughters, Princess Rat-a-Tat-Tat, claimed the throne, proclaimed herself queen, and replaced the men in her father's court with women.

THE LOCKHORNS

Several centuries of civil strife, violence, and war followed, according to Professor Kapliwatsky. Homosexuality became fashionable among all classes in the queendom. Divorce became commonplace. Riots regularly paralyzed the nation's schools and universities. Madmen and drunks abounded in the caves in the hills surrounding the cities. Bandits and robbers reveled day and night, and no man was safe in his home. Women, young and old, were assaulted and raped in broad daylight on the streets of Tabboola, and few citizens came to their aid. Much of the queendom's budget went to the construction of mental institutions, nursing homes, and prisons and to maintain a large police force. The rest of the budget went to wage war with Tabboola's neighbors. From 110 A.D., when Princess Rat-a-Tat-Tat declared herself queen, to 347 A.D., Tabboola's army waged twenty-three wars, losing most of them. The end came when the final war completely decimated its manhood, and the barbarians poured in from the north, pillaging, looting, and raping.

Comparative Madness Factors of Matriarchies, Matri-Patriarchies and Patriarchies

By our calculations—that is, Professor Kapliwatsky's and mine—the Tabboolan civilization, at the height of its glory under old King Tut-a-Tut-Tut, had a madness factor (MF) of 1.1, the lowest of any civilization in history.

Figure 3 is a list of the madness factors of a select group of modern-day patriarchies, matriarchies, and matri-patriarchies (i.e., patriarchies en route to becoming matriarchies), in order of descending madness, as calculated through the algebraic formula representing Samra's Law (Figure 2).

FIGURE 3

The Samra Scale

Madness Factors in Various Patriarchies, Matriarchies, and Matri-Patriarchies

Country	Type of Family Structure	Madness Factor (MF)
Communist China	Matriarchal	17.1
Soviet Union	Matriarchal	14.6
Cuba	Matriarchal	14.2
United States	Matriarchal	13.8
East Germany	Matriarchal	11.4
West Germany	Matriarchal	10.7
Syria	Matriarchal	10.6
Israel	Matriarchal	10.4
Sweden	Matriarchal	9.2
France	Matriarchal	7.6
England	Matriarchal	6.3
Brazil	Matri-patriarchal	2.6
India	Matri-patriarchal	2.2
Japan	Matri-patriarchal	1.9
Portugal	Patriarchal	1.8
Italy	Patriarchal	1.7
Greece	Patriarchal	1.7
Spain	Patriarchal	1.6
Lebanon	Patriarchal	1.5
Malaysia	Patriarchal	1.4
Ceylon	Patriarchal	1.3
Switzerland	Patriarchal	1.3
Aborigines, W. Australia	Patriarchal	1.2
Ancient Tabboola	Patriarchal	1.1

The statistics in Figure 3 show, beyond the shadow of a doubt, the truth of Samra's Law. These figures clearly indicate that patriarchies have the lowest madness factors, followed by matri-patriarchies. After the matri-patriarchies, the MF's among the matriarchies jump enormously, so that by the time we reach matriarchies like the United States, the Soviet Union, and Communist China, the MF's have become thirteen, fourteen, and seventeen times that of ancient Tabboola's.

It should also be noted that none of the societies from the Aborigines of Western Australia to Sweden, with MF's ranging from 1.2 to 9.2, is currently engaged in war or afflicted with any major civil disorders of revolution. Those countries, however, whose MF's exceed 10—the two Germanys, the United States, Cuba, the Soviet Union, Communist China, Syria, Israel—have been beset by foreign wars and/or internal strife in recent decades.

A corollary to Samra's Law, then, is that once a matri-patriarchy or a matriarchy passes the MF 10 mark on the Samra Scale, it stands on the brink of either a foreign war, a civil war, a revolution, riots, civil disorders, or all of these. And nothing—economic prosperity, jobs for all, an efficient police force, two cars in every garage, a chicken in every pot—can keep the nation whose time has come from plunging into chaos.

The Hawkish Matriarchies

As can be seen in Figure 3, matriarchal Communist China has an MF of 17.1, the highest on our scale. In a few short decades China was transformed by the Communist revolution from a relatively serene patriarchy into a bloodthirsty, saber-rattling matriarchy at war or at odds with almost every one of the neighbors on its borders—with Imperial Japan, with capitalist South Korea, with socialist South Vietnam, with socialist India, and even with Communist Russia.

THE LOCKHORNS

"I WISH YOU'D STOP INTRODUCING ME AS YOUR OPPONENT!"

There was a time, not so long ago, when the Chinese were regarded as a peaceful, good-natured, serene, wise, and unflappable race. You can still find elements of this old China in New York's Chinatown, if you look hard enough. Writing recently in the *Journal of Social Psychology*, Richard T. Sollenberger of Mount Holyoke College observed that despite the fact that Chinatown is an overcrowded, run-down, low-income area, it has virtually no delinquency. Sollenberger points out that the Chinese lead stable family lives and have little divorce. Their women, he noted, honor their men. But in the old country things have changed rather dramatically.

If anyone supposes that Chairman Mao is now in control of Red China, he is greatly deluded. Consider the words of *New York Times* correspondent Charles Mohr, reporting recently on the growing influence of Mao's wife, Chiang Ching, who he says has gained control of the cultural revolution: "Mrs. Mao's anger and sharp tongue [have] brought the political destruction of many of the most influential men in China," reports Mohr. Mrs. Mao was reported to have used up "two tons of paper" revising a Chinese opera she didn't like. Tillman Durdin, another *Times* correspondent, reports from Hong Kong that Mrs. Mao was instrumental in reshaping theatrical works to serve political needs. "The new productions," writes Durdin, "emphasize military struggle and glorify the armed forces."

The Soviet Union follows Communist China on the MF scale, and one wonders whether the revolution, wars, and violence that have plagued Russia for more than a century are really better explained by Marxian economics and class conflict than by Russia's cataclysmic transformation from a patriarchy to a matriarchy. All the news reports from matriarchal Russia indicate that the Soviets are suffering from an epidemic of precisely the same social ailments that afflict the United States. On a population percentage basis, Figure 1 (A Statistical View of the American Matriarchy), with few exceptions, could also probably pass very well as an accurate reflection of what is going on in the Soviet Union.

Professor U. Sidorenko writes in *Komsomolskaya Pravda* that the Soviet Union is having growing problems with divorce and broken homes which result in "new cases of hooliganism, drunkenness, juvenile delinquency, vandalism, violence, and other social ills." In Russia, as in the United States, one out of four marriages ends in divorce. One survey shows that Russian men are balking at crushing alimony payments, and that they are complaining because their women want to work outside the home. The woman writer Yelena Andreyeva complains, "How can a boy respect a girl as equal, how can they go on to achieve 'true Communist relations,' if girls are shunted into homemaking classes and not allowed to develop their muscles?" Ex-ballerina Vecheslova appeals to Russian men to help women with household chores at the same time that *Literaturnaya Gazeta* complains that Soviet boys are becoming effeminate because they don't have male teachers.

THE LOCKHORNS

"I KNOW THERE'S NO PLACE LIKE HOME.........
THAT'S WHY I'M HERE!"

An indication of what things have come to in the Soviet Union was provided by a recent letter to the editor of *The Times* from Anya Trofimova Skrok, a Russian woman who fled to the United States. She wrote: "When I read the February 4 news article about the young women who want to be 'liberated,' I wondered what monstrous yoke it is from which they desire liberation. Do they think America, husbands, children, homes, love, and warmth such terrible goals? . . . I think of the young woman who describes herself as a 'Trotskyite Communist' and I wonder if she can understand the supreme state of male-female equality in the Communist state. I do. I worked for four years at Verchne Udinsk in a railroad repair gang beside fourteen men. We were seventeen women. Some of the time we worked for days in water to our knees. We were all equal. I am proud to be a woman in America. I pity these fine young ladies who are so young and so gifted and so unhappy."

It is rather a curious irony that both Israel and Syria, two matriarchies which have been slugging it out for more than two decades, are both high and close together on the MF scale. Professor Kapliwatsky, a Zionist of long standing, deplores the fact that Israel has returned to everything in the Levant except the great patriarchal traditions of Moses, Isaiah, and Amos. He observes, with great sorrow, that the most truculent hawk in Israel is not Moshe Dayan but Golda Meir, and that the only doves in Israel appear to be men.

Nathan Yalin-Mor, the former leader of the terrorist Stern Gang in Israel, has now become a leading proponent of Arab-Israeli reconciliation. He regards Golda Meir as far too hawkish. "She is stubborn, narrow-minded, and vengeful," he says. When results of Israel's Man of the Year poll were published in February, 1971, Golda Meir won with 31 percent of the vote. Defense Minister Moshe Dayan received 22 percent.

As for Syria, Professor Kapliwatsky notes the striking resemblance between the shrill, hysterical, purple propaganda of the Syrians against Israel and that emanating from matriarchal China towards the West. Not long ago, he observes, the Syrians began to promote a socialist organization "for the emancipation of Arab women," formed with the aim of "giving Arab women the chance to share in the Arab and international struggle for liberation." Since then, the Syrians appear to be becoming increasingly truculent. Indeed, the tempo of the fighting in the Middle East has picked up enormously since the Arab nations began recruiting female guerrillas, and the propaganda on both sides is nothing short of bloodthirsty.

THE LOCKHORNS

"WHAT A NIGHTMARE! I DREAMT YOU WERE TWINS!"

Professor Kapliwatsky notes that the three least warlike Arab countries, those least belligerent towards Israel, are Lebanon, Tunisia, and Saudi Arabia, all three of them patriarchies. He believes that the Arabs will never make peace with Israel as long as Golda Meir is premier. He pleads for Israel to return to its patriarchal traditions as the surest path to peace. He is hopeful that if the Israelis get rid of Mrs. Meir and if the more belligerent Arab leaders stop heeding the advice of their hawkish wives, then peace may yet come to this troubled area.

It should also be noted that Indochina and North Vietnam were serene, relatively peaceful countries before the Communists came with promises to emancipate their women. Even so, the delicate Vietnamese women have not been so masculinized as to lose their power to charm American soldiers. A recent study by two U.S. army psychiatrists, as reported in *The Times*, indicated that a significant proportion of American servicemen who marry Vietnamese girls tend to be divorced or afraid of American women. The American woman, the psychiatrists reported, was seen by these servicemen as "aggressive," "demanding," "domineering," "only interested in money and position," "taking too much for granted." To these men, the Vietnamese girls were seen as "kind," "compassionate," "sincere," and "generous." How long this will continue under the Communists is anyone's guess.

The other matriarchies on the MF scale, Sweden, England, and France, are also experiencing precisely the same difficulties. The Swedish woman is one of the most emancipated in the Western world, and Sweden also has one of the highest divorce rates as well as the highest alcoholism and suicide rates in the world. In England, a study of two thousand British executives showing symptoms of stress at the office found that 60 percent of them attributed their conditions to problems at home. Another study showed that one-third of absenteeism in British industry is caused by domestic arguments between workers and their wives.

In France women now enjoy almost as much legal freedom

as their husbands. But France too has been in one war and out of another in this, the feminist century. Indeed, France was a virtual matriarchy when it crumbled under attack by Hitler's armies, and this fact, more than anything else, may have caused its humiliating defeat.

In *The Fall of France* William L. Shirer records that shortly before the German invasion the two mistresses of the two rival French leaders, Premier Paul Reynaud and Edouard Daladier, were dominating their lives and in fact exercising the greatest political power behind the scenes. Reynaud's illness, Shirer says, gave his mistress, the Countess Hélène de Portes, "an opportunity to take temporary control of the affairs of state" on April 27, 1940. Daladier's mistress, the Marquise Jeanne de Crussol, was described by the biographer André Maurois as "a beautiful woman . . . with a taste for power and an unfortunate passion for economic and political doctrines"—about which, apparently, she knew very little.

During this period when France faced its greatest external challenge, the country was, in effect, in the hands of women. And when Shirer entered Paris, the fallen capital, on June 17, he noted in his diary: "I have a feeling that what we're seeing here is the complete breakdown of French society—a collapse of the army, of government, of the morale of the people."

Into France marched an army led by a paranoid bachelor, reputed to be impotent, who all his life had been unable to establish a tender, enduring relationship with a woman. Many of his storm troopers were led by homosexuals and un-balanced neurotics. And according to Joachim C. Fest, Hitler was planning to give holders of the German Cross, the Knight's Cross, and the Iron Cross the right to take a second wife. The fighter, Hitler declared, is entitled to the most beautiful women. "Fighting and love belong together. The bourgeois can think himself lucky to get what is left over."

Is it possible that the tensions within nations and among nations may be caused not so much by economics, politics, nationalism, or class warfare, but simply by the age-old conflicts between male and female? Do these private affairs, when multiplied several millions of times, spill over into conflicts between nations? As Professor Kapliwatsky says, a man who is at peace in his home is not likely to be at war with the world.

The Matri-Patriarchies

Returning to Figure 3, we should also take note that there is a sizable drop in the madness factors from the patriarchies to the matri-patriarchies (patriarchies en route to becoming matriarchies), as here represented by Brazil, India, and Japan.

THE LOCKHORNS

" YES, MOTHER····I TOLD HIM IF HE TOOK ANOTHER DROP IN THIS HOUSE, I'D LEAVE!"

India has an MF of only 2.2 and Japan, 1.9, though it was discovered that the *rate* of increase in the MF's was greater in the matri-patriarchies than in either the matriarchies or the patriarchies. This phenomenon is not wholly explicable, since there are so many variables at work here. However, in some respects, there is more internal tension in a matri-patriarchy than in a matriarchy.

India is a case in point. Long a patriarchal bulwark, traditional Hindu life has been crumbling under the impact of Western culture. Along with their cavalry, the British also brought their feminists, and India has never been the same since. The eminent English psychiatrist William Sargant recently observed that the incidence of psychiatric disorders in India is very low as compared with the West. However, the Indians are starting to catch up and, with the increasing emancipation of their women, they are beginning to be plagued with the same social and psychological disorders that are epidemic in the West.

Until 1954 divorce was alien to Hindu tradition. At that time it became permitted by law, and now the divorce rates are starting to soar. Once known as a serene, gentle, philosophical people, at peace with themselves and with the world (India hadn't started a war for centuries), the Indians, since their feminists began to have their way and Mrs. Gandhi was elected Prime Minister, have become perplexed and grieved by the violence that periodically erupts across the land. The riots *only appear* to be political. Once, while Mrs. Gandhi was speaking before a crowd during a political campaign, she was struck in the face by a rock—the sort of thing that was unheard of in old India. And, of a sudden, we see the strange spectacle of the pacific Indians sending their army to invade the Portuguese colonies, clamoring for a showdown with the

Chinese on their northern borders, and exchanging threats with Pakistan.

The Indian politicians are now fond of quoting an old Sanskrit saying, in regards to Mrs. Gandhi: You may see a crow with white feathers or a fish with feet, but you will never understand the mind of a woman.

Japan, another matri-patriarchy, is also undergoing cataclysmic changes. The Japanese would probably readily forgive us for defeating them so badly in World War II if it weren't for the fact that we also forced our feminist notions on this ancient race. Japanese women consider the constitution devised and installed by the United States occupation forces as their emancipation proclamation. The Americans insisted on giving the Japanese women the vote and also the right to initiate a divorce and get alimony, and Japan hasn't been quite the same since. Japanese women, whom World War II GIs remember with nostalgia, have taken to politics, and the divorce rate is steadily increasing. The traditional pattern of Japanese home life is breaking up.

Still, a measure of patriarchal sanity reigns in Japan. Tokyo is one of the world's safest cities, and women can walk the streets at night without fear. And according to a recent study by the community council of greater New York, alcoholism is practically nonexistent in Japan. Though Alcoholics Anonymous chapters have multiplied throughout the matriarchies of the world, AA has made no inroads in Japan. The seven groups around Tokyo were all formed by Westerners. However, things are changing rapidly, and Japan has yet to experience the full consequences of its conquest by the American matriarchy.

So distressed by the Westernization and womanization of Japan was the brilliant Japanese novelist Yukio Mishima, that he stunned Japan recently by committing hara-kiri in the presence of a commanding general and several of his followers. A friend of Mishima for twenty years, Edward Seidensticker, professor of Far Eastern languages at the University of Michigan, told me that the author "thought modern Japan was essentially womanish, and he wanted Japan to return to its masculine tradition." That was not reported in the American press.

The Peaceful Patriarchies

The MF factors among the patriarchies listed in Figure 3 range from a modest 1.1 for ancient Tabboola to 1.8 for Portugal. Portugal, one of the last bastions of male supremacy, is a country which has not been at war with its neighbors for several centuries. The only semblance of a suffragette movement in this peaceful country appeared after World War II, but was quickly stamped out as subversive. Recently the beginnings of a feminist movement have been forming, but the new civil code of Portugal reaffirms the position of the husband as the head of the family.

Patriarchal Italy has the lowest juvenile delinquency rate of any country in the Western world, according to no less an authority than Judge Samuel S. Leibowitz of Brooklyn's criminal court. Of patriarchal Greece, Stephanos Zotos writes: "Modern Greek men demand and get from women what they want. Masculine domination in Greece is an indisputable fact. Greek men seem to possess a charisma to which Greek and foreign women have been and are continuing to be attracted. Many Greek men will tell you that their women are much happier than, for example, American women. They believe that American women are frustrated because, in their efforts to gain equal rights with men, they have lost the charm of their femininity. While there has been a slight erosion in the supreme male position . . . there is no real national feminist movement. Most Greek women—the most intelligent, as far as the Greek men are concerned—hope that the present inequality of the sexes prevails forever. Their acceptance of masculine supremacy makes them feel more feminine, or so they say. And their men feel more manly.

"The Greeks do not speak openly about their private lives. They are discreet. They do not speak or read about or discuss sex; they confess they only practice it. They believe that it is not for the psychiatrists or the sociologists to analyze the issue and its effects on the life of a human being."

In patriarchal Ceylon, which has a remarkably low MF of 1.3, there is only *one* mental institution serving the entire country. Dr. C. Fernando, a Ceylonese psychiatrist at the United Nations, explained to me that "this is not because we cannot afford another one, but because there isn't a need for it." Ceylon hasn't been at war with anyone for centuries, either.

Patriarchal Lebanon's MF is a modest 1.5. I visited my parents' native land a dozen years ago as a newspaperman and found the Lebanese to be, on the whole, a good-humored, friendly, and unwarlike, though decidedly shrewd, race of people. About the same time, President Eisenhower sent marines to Lebanon to quell "a civil war" which turned out to be nothing more than a family feud. Our troops were astonished when they were greeted on the beaches not by Communist revolutionaries and guerillas, but by an army of Lebanese hawkers selling popcorn, chewing gum, peanuts, Cokes, and *Playboy* magazines.

Lebanon has only *one* mental institution serving the whole of the country. And when one of my Lebanese cousins, a psychiatrist who had studied and trained in America, returned to Beirut to set up a private practice, he couldn't find enough business to support himself. He thereupon returned to the States, and at last report is prospering. He is a fine psychiatrist. I wish him well.

THE LOCKHORNS

"....AND I'D SUGGEST THAT HEREAFTER YOU BOTH REFRAIN FROM CALLING EACH OTHER DUM-DUM AND YO-YO!"

Switzerland, a patriarchy which until recently had not given its women the vote, has been one of the most peaceful countries in the world. Switzerland stayed out of both World War I and World War II. Its MF is an extremely low 1.3. It is a country remarkably free from violence, riots, and crime. One would be hard put to name the last time that Switzerland was involved in a civil war or a war with its neighbors. In February, 1971, Swiss women won the right to vote in federal elections in a referendum. It shall be interesting now to observe how long it will take for Switzerland to develop the same social ailments and massive military machines that have overwhelmed other emancipated states.

The modern-day patriarchy with the lowest MF, second only to that of ancient Tabboola, is located on a small island off the coast of Western Australia and is inhabited by Aborigines who, according to Henry W. H. Butler, rate their women after their hunting dogs in their social order. The men rate first, the children next, the hunting dogs third, and the women fourth. This patriarchy has an MF, by our calculations, of 1.2. The island has no mental institutions, prisons, courts, police, juvenile homes, reformatories, or nursing homes. And everyone appears to be quite happy.

Samra's Phenomenon

Another phenomenon, related to Samra's Law, I shall call Samra's Phenomenon, and that is:

Normal people who move from a patriarchy to a matriarchy are likely, in time, to become unhinged. Crazy people who move from a matriarchy to a patriarchy are likely to regain their minds.

Thus the young Lawrence Durrell who wrote *The Black Book*, a study in madness, lost his balance in matriarchal England and recovered it only after fleeing to patriarchal Greece. T. E. Lawrence lost his sanity in matriarchal England, recovered it in patriarchal Arabia, and lost it again when he returned to England.

Some parts of India, they say, still work their magic healing powers. In a New York hospital several years ago, I met a charming young Indian named Rao who was then recovering from a nervous breakdown. He had been in America for several years, and neither Yoga, the *Gita*, nor the *Kama Sutra* could teach him how to live in peace with American women. Eight years of knowing, marrying, and divorcing them had exhausted and unmanned him. After his discharge from the hospital he returned to India, and the next time I heard from him he announced that he had married an Indian girl from a small village in Punjab. This time he had asked his parents to select his bride for him, and the letter he wrote me waxed ecstatically about her.

"She has never been beyond grammar school," he wrote, "but this does not overly distress me, as I believe that a superstitious woman is less dangerous than an educated one, and that an ignorant woman is certainly less of a problem than a misinformed one . . .

"Of course," he went on, "she is a virgin. All the women here are expected to be virgins on their wedding day. I think you may come to see that virginity in women has several decided advantages. For one, it promotes social order. Moreover, she is not likely to torture me as the other three did with daily comparisons with past boyfriends, lovers, fiancés, and husbands."

He concluded: "I know that you will think our custom strange of having the parents select one's wife. But if you could see Leela, and if you would have known my first three wives, then you could not help but agree that my parents' taste is far superior to my own. She serves me night and day, and life is good again."

One wonders too why all those old English empire-builders—Gordon, Lawrence, et al—came alive in patriarchies like Greece, Arabia, the Sudan, India, China? And why did they always dislike so much being reassigned to the motherland?

Why were the Huxleys fascinated with India? And why did that old social agitator J. B. S. Haldane end up his life serenely in India, wrapped in a white robe?

The truth of Samra's Law, as well as of Samra's Corollary and Samra's Phenomenon, is self-evident and requires no further proof. However, for those who remain skeptical, Professor Kapliwatsky is prepared to provide, upon request, additional historical materials, statistics, charts, and graphs, as well as assistance in calculating the madness factor of any country, past or present. And for those who, with a scientific bent of mind, require still additional proof, I refer you to the letters and communications to the Society for the Emancipation of the American Male, which provide further evidence of the truth of Samra's Law.

THE LOCKHORNS

"MARRIAGE IS A TWO-WAY STREET, SAM·····
THEY GET YOU COMING AND GOING!"

In the final chapter of this tract, I propose to advance Samra's Principle, which suggests how some civilizations in decline have risen to the threat of the feminist hordes and recovered their manhood. And since, besides being a historian of great perception, I am also clairvoyant, I shall conclude with Samra's Prophecy. But first, allow me to examine with you in more depth, dear reader, the woman question and its relationship to the madness and violence of our times.

For those of you who cannot be persuaded of the truth even with scientific evidence and argument, I ask you, in all humility, to accept Samra's Law on faith, for the time being, at all events. For faith is a man, and doubt is a woman.

Women
and Madness

Not long after the formation of the Society for the Emancipation of the American Male, we received the following communication from the husband of a famous feminist:

"Count me in. Two men in a family are just too many.

           —Good luck"

Several weeks later, another letter arrived from this gentleman, now the former husband of a famous feminist:

"Incidentally," he wrote, "I am no longer married to ———. We are legally separated after several agonizing years of trying to get disentangled. No feminist is ever happily married unless she marries an eunoch [sic]."

Thereafter, one letter after another began arriving from persons who blamed their psychiatric problems on women. Wrote one man from the Diagnostic and Treatment Center in

Dannemora, New York: "I am a chronic criminal offender whose biggest problem is my relations with women. I am incarserated [sic] in a therapeutic community of an experimental nature wherein these problems are explored. I am incapable of handling my mother, but am trying to overcome the problem I have with my wife. The help I need is tremendous and the reason I am writing is my plea for any assistance you can give me. Allow me to take this opportunity to congratulate you on a noble and extremely worthwhile venture."

THE LOCKHORNS

"OF COURSE, THE LOCKHORNS DO HAVE SOMETHING IN COMMON·····AN UNBRIDLED HATRED OF EACH OTHER!"

Another man, a messenger from God, sent to save us, was locked up en route. "I aggree [sic] heartily with your views," he wrote from Lakewood, Colorado. "I was supposed to have brought the overthrow of female equality way back in 1955, as I was the messenger that God had sent to come to the rescue of America. But I was attacked by a psychiatrist in a veterans hospital, and he succeeded in damaging my soul, which rendered me unfit to serve God anymore. That's why there has been no one on the American scene these past confusing years."

One gentleman, writing from St. Louis, observed that "The Bible is very plain on women being under subjection and not working . . . This so-called women's sufferage [sic] was a plan to demoralize the people by the international bankers, and the politicians are two-fold children of the devel [sic]. Most politicians ought to burn in hell, and will when they die. The morals of America have been going down ever since the 1920 Amendment giving women the vote."

A lady realtor from Denver wrote: "I am with you and would like to join your Ladies' Auxiliary. I am getting a divorce after 33 years of marriage, and most of it was due to a weak male figure and my being turned into a man, of necessity. I endorse your campaign to teach women to be better wives and mothers. The American woman is desperate for help, and I see none forthcoming except yours."

A young lady wrote from Menlo Park, California: "I am a young woman recently separated from a medical student-husband who feels very much a victim of the very thing you are fighting against in America today. Nothing relieves me more than to know that there are still male-men in the world who appreciate being that way and can handle the situation accordingly. My upbringing was one in which the male influence was totally bleak and ugly—misleading and frustrating. My father, a very weak and sensitive man, was alcoholic and totally unequipped to handle the family situation. My mother naturally took the reins (I cannot judge at this point whether she took them from him or whether she took them because he relinquished them) but whatever the pattern, it made a mess of four children's lives.

"When I married my husband, I hoped for, in him, much of what I never received through a father-daughter relationship, but I suppose the way my personality had been shaped was just too much for the both of us. Bringing in the major source of income for the family didn't help the situation either. In your attempts to better the position of the American male, I strongly urge that you consider the working-wife, student-husband situation because in so many cases this is where manliness begins to degenerate and probably the major reason is the wife who begins to feel too independent. I certainly hope that something can be done for the boys growing up now, the homosexuals who fear women because of bad experiences with them, and all the young men like my husband. I would have benefited from an effort like yours a very long time ago."

A member of the Mattachine Society of New York, a homosexual organization, wrote asking for our support and asked us, "Would you want your daughter to marry a heterosexual?"

Marie Anderson, women's editor of *The Miami Herald*, sent us an article her newspaper ran on the problems likely to be encountered by those changing sex, particularly from male to female. The article on transsexuals quoted Dr. Richard Green, a psychiatrist who is director of the gender identity research and treatment center at the University of California medical school, as saying that, generally, three to four males for every female want to switch sexes.

Not a few psychiatrists, psychologists and doctors hailed the formation of the Society. Wrote Dr. Laurence J. Peter, the eminent psychologist and author of *The Peter Principle*: "My gratitude to you for the formation of such a noble enterprise. It is an honor to join such a worthwhile cause.

There have been many warnings. Phillip Wylie's *Generation of Vipers*, Roth's *Portnoy's Complaint*, and now Lionel Tiger's *Men In Groups*. All give us pause to consider the fate of the human race. May we avoid The Final Placement Syndrome!"

Dr. Arthur H. Cain, another psychologist and author of *Young People and Neurosis*, joined SEAM and declared: "I have for many years attempted to awaken the American Male (not Man) to the fact that the greatest single threat to Western civilization is the American Woman—so far without much success. I am with you 100 percent on your new movement."

THE LOCKHORNS

"THE LOCKHORNS ARE DUE AT NINE-THIRTY.
HERE ARE YOUR TRANQUILIZERS."

Dr. Walter C. Alvarez, professor-emeritus of the Mayo Foundation and syndicated columnist, wrote: "Hooray for you! As a physician, I have been much interested in the fact that males are more subject to many diseases than are females. I once had one of my students go through the literature to find diseases which usually affect women more than men, and he found a few, such as gall bladder disease. Many other diseases such as duodenal ulcer and cancer of the stomach appear usually three times as often in men as in women. A woman has a life expectancy some five years greater—as I remember—than have men. That is one reason why there are so many widows, and why, I am told, three-fourths of the wealth of this country is in the hands of widows. Every so often one sees a widow who has had two or more husbands die . . ."

An instructor in psychiatry wrote from California: "You are quite right that where men rule the home, there is little, if any neurosis. In point of fact, as women have assumed, or been given, more and more 'rights' (outside of the feminine role), we have far more women seeking absolution from the very psychiatrists who condone unisex."

Richard Milan, executive director of the National Council on Alcoholism, greater Phoenix area, observed that "counseling both male and female alcoholics repeatedly reveals indistinct sexual identification and identity crises. I have a happy suspicion that you're on the right track."

Dr. K. Schmidt of the Department of Behavioral Science at Southern Colorado State College, sent along the following passage from a recent book called *Hominology*, written by Professor Theodore C. Kahn, his department chairman:

"In their inability to cope with a world which no longer finds them essential, the fathers of our time again become little boys; and we read about 'bringing up father' as if it were the most natural thing in the world to all but diaper an adult. Some fathers react to this by assuming the role of clowns within their family circle; others attempt futilely to re-establish their former roles as tyrants; some try to be good little boys, as in 'good old Dad,' but a growing number resort to alcohol to drown their shame. Many attempt to demonstrate their masculinity in a variety of inappropriate ways, but a sizable percentage simply drop dead from heart attacks as the least complicated way out of the dilemma . . .

"It might be of interest to wives to note that most males require a feeling of dominance to retain their sexual vigor . . . Some (as yet unsubstantiated) research suggests that a feeling of dominance among males tends to prolong their lives. If true, this also could be explained as having survival value for the species. Women who fail to give their mates the vital sense of dominance they need and who are unable to pretend that they are being saved and nurtured by their frustrated males, abet and intensify their husband's problems . . ."

NIM Grant No. 211: The Impotent Sex Researchers

In 1960, A. Abdullah, S. El-Mutwalli, M. Abu Nasser, K. Hassan, and S. Goldberg secured a $750,000 grant from the National Institute of Madness to study the sex lives of male sex researchers. The survey by Abdullah et al., done over a span of ten years, unearthed the startling fact that, of 788 male sex researchers studied, 77.6 percent of them were impotent, and another 43.2 percent were divorced. In addition, biochemists working independently discovered a strange substance in the blood of the majority of sex researchers, not found in the serum of normals. The normals were used as a control group. The strange substance, discovered in orthomolecular amounts, had the following structural formula similar to that of the drug Tetrahydrocannabinal:

$$CH_3H\ H \quad \overset{H}{\underset{}{O}}$$

Tetrahydrocannabinol

What this means is not certain at this time, but researchers feel this is an important clue which is likely to lead to a major breakthrough.

THE LOCKHORNS

"I'VE HAD A NAGGING PAIN FOR YEARS."

It was not long after this study was completed that we received news from St. Louis that Elisabeth Masters, the wife of the eminent sex researcher Dr. William H. Masters, had been granted a divorce. Mrs. Masters had sought the divorce on the grounds of desertion, and the judge ordered Dr.

Masters to pay $2,038 monthly in alimony. Masters is a co-author of the best-selling book *Human Sexual Inadequacy*. A few months later, Dr. Masters and his coresearcher, Virginia Johnson, another divorcée, announced that they had gotten married.

It has been said, and I believe a lady psychoanalyst by the name of Marynia Farnham said it, "the more educated the woman is, the greater chance there is of sexual disorder, more or less severe." And Margaret Mead, in one of her rare enlightened moments, has observed that "no human gift is strong enough to flower fully in a person who is threatened with loss of sex membership."

Dr. George Albee, retired president of the American Psychological Association, told the association at its recent convention: "The typical psychiatric patient is a college-educated, white, upper-middle-class, non-Catholic female between thirty and forty who is either anxious because she's not married or anxious because she is."

The U.S. Public Health Service recently reported evidence suggesting that one in five American adults has experienced a nervous breakdown or felt one coming on. Unexpectedly, the Public Health Service reported lower rates of breakdown among persons who had never married.

Drs. Robert L. Dupont, Jr., and Henry Grunebaum recently published the results of a remarkable study they made in *The American Journal of Psychiatry*. The article was published under the self-explanatory title, "Willing Victims: The Husbands of Paranoid Women." The husbands were all found to be normal.

Though this was not one of its objectives, the feminist movement has led to the steady erosion of the mental and physical health of the men and children of America. Parents

Without Partners is an organization which tries to help single parents cope with child-rearing and being alone. It has a membership of 50,000 single parents and 150,000 children. According to Dan Isaacson, president of the Manhattan chapter of Parents Without Partners, "It's very common for the children of single parents to be in some sort of therapy or other."

"Extreme feminists," says Dr. Abram Kardiner, former chief of the Department of Psychiatry at Columbia, "shouldn't undertake to become mothers. You can't pay anyone to love your child. The monogamous family is the perfect environment for child development, for the incubation of feelings. I think you're dealing with dynamite when you toy with it. From what I've seen of the liberationists, their most conspicuous feature is self-hatred. I see tremendous vituperativeness and lack of feeling. They think it's a curse to be female and have exaggerated opinions about the merits of being a male."

Says Dr. Nathan Ackerman of the Family Institute of New York: "I am a Jew whose character, way of life, personal values, and choice of professional pursuit have been molded by the Jewish family tradition of loyalty and mutual aid . . . In my field of work, the evidence is clear: the fate of the individual and his family are organically intertwined and interdependent . . . Look around you. How many families do you know that are normal and healthy? For every married couple that enters the divorce courts, there are uncounted numbers that remain under one roof and yet continue in the chronic agony of emotional divorce. The incidence of mental illness, delinquency, and addiction in divorced alienated persons is conspicuously higher than in stable families. The rate of suicide is three times as high."

Dr. Konrad Lorenz, author of the book *On Aggression*, argues that large and stable family groupings are essential to the survival of human society. Says Dr. Lorenz: "The survival of society at all—of human society—is in doubt, particularly if the family structure is not kept up. I believe that the innate program of the human individual is such that he cannot deploy all his possibilities and evolve all his inherent faculties unless it's done within the frame of the normal family."

Many psychiatrists and psychologists have expressed concern that homosexuality has reached "almost epidemic proportions." The Committee on Public Health of the New York Academy of Medicine, after a thorough investigation, declared recently that homosexuality is "an illness of social proportions, national significance, and serious portent." Perhaps significantly, most homosexuals are reluctant homosexuals. When three hundred homosexuals were asked by the Mattachine Society, "If you had a son, would you want him to be a homosexual?" only six answered yes.

The Canadian psychiatrist Daniel Cappon says that "the natural history of the homosexual person seems to be one of frigidity, impotence, broken personal relationships, psychosomatic disorders, alcoholism, paranoid psychosis (i.e., the mental illness of suspicion and persecution) and suicide." Dr. Lawrence J. Hatterer of the Payne Whitney Psychiatric Clinic in New York City, author of *Changing Homosexuality In the Male*, lists many causes, nearly all of them beginning with some form of unhappy home life in childhood. He estimates that about 20 million American men practice some form of homosexuality. "Let's face it," says Dr. Hatterer, "for a young boy who wants sex, it's much easier and faster and often less threatening to make a homosexual contact than to pick up a girl."

Peter and Barbara Wyden, in their book *Growing Up Straight,* describe the strange case of a young boy who became a homosexual in the United States. Curiously, when he traveled to Europe, heterosexual relations posed no problems for him, but as soon as he came back to the States he resumed his homosexuality.

Sociologist Judson T. Landis questioned eighteen hundred college students and discovered that a third of them had had experience with at least one sexual deviate. In the case of men, 84 percent of these episodes represented a homosexual approach.

THE LOCKHORNS

"HERE COMES LOCKHORN. NEITHER SNOW NOR RAIN NOR GLOOM OF NIGHT SHALL KEEP HIM FROM HIS APPOINTED ROUNDS."

The eminent psychologist Dr. Paul Popenoe, president of the American Institute of Family Relations, observes that homosexuality "has long been recognized as often associated with fear or hatred for the female sex . . . In spite of all the bluster and bragging of homosexual propagandists, the litera-

ture is filled with pictures of their frustration and misery."
What is needed, according to Dr. Popenoe, is "a widespread
and vigorous campaign to promote successful marriage and
teach parents how to rear children correctly."

James Reston, the distinguished columnist of *The New
York Times* and a man who has long felt that a woman's
place is in the home, expressed alarm recently over the de-
generation of the American male's mental and physical
health. "What has surprised the President [Nixon] and his
principal aides and recruiters," Reston wrote, "is how many
times they have considered prominent men with established
reputations, only to discover after careful investigation some
physical or psychological weakness that disqualified the man
for the job. 'I had never realized,' one Cabinet member
remarked the other day, 'what a toll the fierce competition
of American business and professional life has taken on many
of our most successful and talented men. Many of them have
simply been worn out in the struggle. Many more have all
kinds of family problems that they cannot leave. In a great
many cases, they have taken to drink . . .' "

Since 1964, surgeons at the University of Michigan
Hospital have transplanted five hearts. Though four of the
heart transplant patients later died, one of them, Donald
Kaminski, age thirty-eight, is still going strong. Recently he
was in Detroit living it up. Kaminski went to a race track,
consumed half a dozen bottles of beer, smoked a few ciga-
rettes, and announced he was forming a new company to sell
portable sauna baths. When Kaminski was interviewed by
reporters at the hospital following his operation a couple
years ago, he declared that he expected to live a long time
because he didn't have a wife to nag him. The four other
heart transplant patients, who didn't survive, were married.

Psychiatric researchers T. Ishiyama and A. F. Brown reported in *The Journal of Clinical Psychology* on their intriguing study of "Sex Role Conceptions and the Patient Role in a State Mental Hospital." The researchers took 120 schizophrenic patients, half of them from open-door good units and the other half from locked-door disturbed units. They found that "successful mental patients proved to be more appropriately masculine or feminine in their self-concepts and ideal concepts than did unsuccessful patients." They found that "successful male patients were more masculine in their self-concepts." They also found that "the self-concept of the unsuccessful males was as feminine as the ideal concepts and self-concepts of the successful females and even more feminine than the self-concept of the unsuccessful females." Successful female patients were also more feminine in their self-concepts than were unsuccessful females.

In his book *Termination: The Closing of Baker Plant*, Alfred H. Slote suggests how important a good wife is in the life of a man. Slote interviewed former employees and executives of a closed Detroit plant to find out what happens to people when a factory closes up and moves away. About 50 percent of the men left jobless, Slote found, were beset by ulcers, arthritis, hypertension, alcoholism, and depression. Those who survived in good health, mentally and physically, had good wives, Slote reported.

From an unlikely source, Patricia Sexton, professor of sociology and education at New York University, and author of *The Feminized Male*, comes this eloquent appeal: "We need tough and courageous men—men who are also men of reason, tolerance, learning, and good will. The shortage of male heroes and the entry into the vacuum of minstrels, musicians, Beatles, Rolling Stones—as well as an assortment of demented anti-heroes—makes it hard to personalize for the young whatever ideals of masculinity we may share . . . The fact that 85% of the public school elementary teachers are women is an important factor. Many women actively dislike and resent males. They take their revenge where they can, in the home and the school, on the young males they control. They both pamper them and punish them. The solution is to remove boys from the jurisdiction of women, and to correct the social injustices that make many women so resentful of men . . . But Mama is only half the problem. The other half is Papa. Papa's absence from home, his abdication of authority to Mama, his weakness, brutality, or failure to relate to his son can also lead to feminization . . ."

The feminists themselves, it appears, have been constitutionally unable to take a long view of their lives and their impact on others. They ride high in the saddle for a time—when they are young and attractive—and then, as they age, they pay the piper. Their husbands frequently abandon them for other women. Along the way, mental institutions and sanitariums beckon. Psychiatrists and lawyers become their constant companions. Oriental women have often noted how quickly American women age. And while the women of patriarchal societies are cherished, honored, and cared for by their husbands and sons as they grow old, in America it has become fashionable to put Mom away in that great American institution—the nursing home, where the unloved and unwanted live out their desperate lives—and everyone breathes a great sigh of relief.

That is liberation?

Four Cases of Male Madness among Preachers and Physicians, and the Confessions of a Former Feminist

In all modesty, it was our clinic, the Samra Clinic for the Study of Incipient and Chronic Madness, that provided us with the most convincing evidence in support of Samra's Law. The Clinic, a nonprofit institution wholly dependent on fund-raisers, was set up in 1963 and ably staffed by some of the finest psychiatrists and psychologists in the world. I am not at liberty to reveal their names at this time. We have deliberately attempted to avoid publicity because of the delicate nature of our work and research.

The clinic was set up to study the causes of insanity as well as to provide an asylum for those persons in public life whose attacks of madness must of necessity be kept a well-guarded secret. Few persons know of our existence. We specialized in treating eminent persons whom we duly registered under false names, and I regret that I cannot at this time reveal the location of the clinic. I ask the reader only to take my word that the clinic does, in fact, exist, and that per annum costs are generally in line with other such clinics and sanitariums— i.e., in the neighborhood of $45,000. (I should like to point out that our administrative and fund-raising costs never exceed 90 percent per annum, and that the balance always goes to research. Contributions are always, of course, welcome.)

THE LOCKHORNS

"AS A MATTER OF FACT MY WIFE **IS** MISSING. WHO'S THE FINK WHO TOLD YOU?"

The most intriguing cases we received at the clinic these past five years were: the owner of a health school, an evangelist, a Christian Science practitioner, and a psychiatrist.

Case No. 50825: *Big George Mussels, Physical Culturist*

Big George Mussels was what is commonly regarded as a health food faddist or nut. He was a confirmed vegetarian and raw-food addict, and lived by all the best health principles. He did not smoke or drink or eat processed foods. He ate nothing but organic foods, refusing anything that had a hint of an insecticide on it. He drank only distilled water. He consumed quantities of yogurt, wheat germ, and black molasses, and every morning he drank a half-gallon of fresh carrot-and-celery juice, made with his own electric juicer. Every day he took several dozen varieties of vitamins and food supplements. He lifted weights every morning and jogged five miles every evening.

Big George—a large, powerful man with rippling muscles—boasted that he had studied under the famous physical culturist Bernarr Macfadden, and at the age of seventy-six he too was sky-diving from airplanes. He was a beautiful specimen of manhood with a ruddy complexion only slightly discolored by the large quantities of carrot juice he insisted on consuming daily. He was able to lift with one hand the rear end of a Volkswagen occupied by four passengers.

At seventy-six, Big George looked fifty. That is, until he met and fell in love with Louisa, a young girl fifty-one years his junior. Big George, a naturopath, ran a health school in Louisiana and had largely avoided women most of his life. Louisa had come to his health school as a patient, suffering from asthma, and he had introduced her to his health secrets. Under his care she had regained much of her health and developed into quite a fetching beauty. Soon Big George was sneaking away every night to see Louisa, and neglecting his sanitarium.

Louisa was a most ambitious young girl, and also a contentious one, and the two fought and quarreled a great deal. The passion of their nights together and the heat of their quarrels soon began to wear on Big George, and it was not long before his patients began to notice that he had lost the spring in his step. He began walking slowly, with his eyes riveted on the floor. His eyes became bloodshot, his complexion pale. His hair began to fall out, and his gums started to bleed. He developed a duodenal ulcer and arthritis in both hands. He complained continually of fatigue and an assortment of aches and pains, and when he finally came to our clinic—surreptitiously after an all-night train ride—he had the emanciated appearance of a victim of starvation. He weighed a mere ninety-eight pounds on our scale, and a strange odor emanated from his being. He came to our clinic in a stupor, held on to the thread of life for a few weeks, and notwithstanding everything modern science could do for him, died with his mouth forming the word "Louisa."

Five years after Big George met Louisa, she buried him. She is now running the health school in Louisiana, which is called Louisa's Health School.

Case No. 11,483: The Reverend Mr. Joseph W. Tremblechin, Evangelist

The Reverend Mr. Joseph W. Tremblechin was a great orator and evangelist. He traveled a hundred thousand miles every year, preaching the gospel and calling sinners to repentance. Wherever he went, he drew large and appreciative crowds. His weekly sermons were carried by 376 radio and television stations throughout the country. His publishing firm, Tremblechin Enterprises, produced inspirational books and pamphlets by the hundreds of thousands. So successful was Tremblechin Enterprises that the firm was reputed to be a multi-million-dollar operation.

Thousands of souls were brought to God through Reverend Tremblechin's dedicated efforts. It was widely supposed that the love of God kept Reverend Tremblechin on the road day and night, traveling through the country. There are those who claim that this is so, and indeed Reverend Tremblechin did love God with all his heart and all his mind and all his soul, and was prepared to answer His call anywhere. But it so happened that there was another reason, and we did not discover it until recently, when the Reverend Tremblechin registered his wife at our clinic—under an assumed name, of course—and vowed us to secrecy lest the word get out.

Mrs. Tremblechin was the daughter of the famous Mr. —— who had built a publishing empire. She was a large, formidable woman with a mouth that sent legions of bilious words marching before her. We found her to be a definition of madness, a classic case of hypergoflugaschmaladia. Her symptoms were kaleidoscopic and were so numerous as to preclude their being listed herein, for want of space. Her blood chemistry was such that our biochemists had not seen anything like it before, and have not seen anything like it since.

Mrs. Tremblechin, one of the first of the suffragettes, prided herself on having been instrumental in the campaign to pass the Nineteenth Amendment giving women the vote, and had—Reverend Tremblechin informed us—spent most of her life going from one psychiatrist's couch to another's. A total of 1,857 electric shock treatments, which we gave her with her husband's permission, failed to silence her. She awoke from each one jabbering endlessly. Tranquilizers helped not at all.

And the Reverend Mr. Tremblechin himself, at his wit's end, confessed that he felt guilt-ridden because thoughts of murder kept bubbling up from his subconscious. He agonized continually over these death wishes, doubting that a wife murderer would be welcome in heaven. In our interviews with him, he confessed, weeping all the while, that he kept on the road lest he succumb to the temptation of finishing off his wife. He allowed that, if it weren't for his wife, he would prefer to give it all up and take a small parish in the countryside.

THE LOCKHORNS

"AND THEN ONE DAY LORETTA'S INCESSANT CHATTER ACTUALLY STARTED MAKING SENSE!"

Reverend Tremblechin, poor man, a gentleman who had saved the souls of many strangers, regarded himself as a failure with his own family. The Tremblechins have three teenage children. One of the sons is considering a sex-change operation. A daughter has become a lady wrestler. And the second son is the drummer in a rock band, in addition to being a drug addict.

Mrs. Tremblechin remains at our clinic. Her prognosis is not good. Her condition is, in fact, hopeless. Reverend Tremblechin is, of course, still traveling and preaching, and curiously, most of his converts appear to be women.

Case No. 8,342: Dr. Wolfgang Witherhead, Psychiatrist and Marriage Counselor

Dr. Wolfgang Witherhead studied under Freud in Vienna, and was one of his most brilliant students. Dr. Witherhead once asked Freud if he believed in equality in marriage. "That is a practical impossibility," replied Freud. "There must be inequality and the superiority of the man is the lesser of two evils." But on this single point Dr. Witherhead disagreed with the master. He became an authority on sex and marriage counseling, adapting the psychoanalytic technique to this ancient art, and soon had a sizable practice.

He taught that equality among marriage partners was the only sensible approach to matrimony and proclaimed what has come to be known as "the balance-of-power theory of marriage," in which he maintained that marital happiness is dependent upon the maintenance of a delicate balance of power between the spouses. Dr. Witherhead later founded the School of Marriage Counseling, Psychoanalyticphysiology, and Gestalt Genetics, which, however, because of feuding in the ranks later split into four schools: the School of Marriage Counseling, the School of Psychoanalysis, the School of Psychophysiology, and the School of Gestalt Genetics. Each school went its own way, and none of the four schools' members would speak to one another thereafter.

Dr. Witherhead was best known, however, for a twenty-year, NIM-funded, $500,000 research study of a thousand hospitalized male schizophrenics, in which he proved that the left toenails of schizophrenics grew at a rate 1.65 times faster than the left toenails of a group of normals. What this meant was not entirely clear at the time, and Dr. Witherhead's findings were widely ridiculed by his colleagues until recent years, when the physiology of schzophrenia began to attract close scientific attention. And now some of his colleagues are beginning to recognize the importance of his work. But, more than anything, Dr. Witherhead was remembered for his famous observation in regards to schizophrenia: "Gentlemen, two heads are not necessarily better than one."

THE LOCKHORNS

"SEPARATE BILLS, PLEASE...."

Dr. Witherhead had originally come to our clinic as a member of our psychiatric staff, but after his fifth wife left him, his nerves snapped and he stayed on as a patient. None of his five marriages lasted more than three years, and each, he confessed, had been turbulent and unendurable. He was a sensitive man, with a philosophical bent, and quite likable. After each divorce he slid into a catatonic condition and sat inflexibly for hours staring blankly at the walls of his room. The condition soon developed into a full-blown case of paranoia, with the wildest of auditory and visual hallucinations. He became convinced that the ancient Furies were pursuing him, were attempting to poison him, and wished to tear him limb from limb and devour him. No amount of shock treatments, tranquilizers, or psychotherapy could shake him from this delusion.

His fifth wife had run off with the promotion manager of *McCall's* magazine, one of the chaps who was at that time promoting togetherness. Dr. Witherhead, poor wretch, was entirely inconsolable and entirely mad. He is still with us, and is likely to be here for some time. In his madness he appears to be finding some comfort in the Book of Isaiah, which is all he is allowing himself to read these days. He sits in his room for hours reading Isaiah, for reasons only he knows, as he does not wish to talk.

Case No. 24,521: Mr. Eddy B. Merry, Christian Science Practitioner

Mr. Eddy B. Merry was a Christian Science practitioner, a jovial and friendly gentleman who nonetheless appeared to be continually suffering from the common cold, in the summertime as well as the wintertime. He would lurch over in a paroxysm of sneezing, and then cheerfully apologize and deny that he was ill. He breathed with difficulty, wheezing on occasion, and it was clear that he was an asthmatic as well. Later, though he went to great lengths to conceal it, we discovered that he also had the gout in the worst sort of way.

"Nothing to it," he would say. "It's all in the mind. All is mind."

When Mr. Merry arrived at our clinic, he was carrying with him under his arm a large portrait of Mary Baker Eddy. He insisted on hanging it in his room, and he would spend hours lying on his bed looking lovingly at the painting.

Mr. Merry was in the midst of a divorce which his wife had initiated, and his nerves had given out under the strain of the court proceedings. His wife was a well-known feminist who had a Ph.D. in psychology and who, like many of the American women of her generation, was rich in knowledge and poor in wisdom. She had carried on affairs with a succession of men and described them in great detail to her husband, which helped to unhinge him.

One of our staff psychiatrists interviewed Mrs. Merry when her husband was admitted to our clinic. She was quite frank: "I have a wonderful husband who is madly in love with me after twelve years of marriage," she wept. "So help me, as a person, as a God-fearing Christian man, he is the greatest. He has just the right amount of all the right qualities. He is kind, affectionate, generous, even-tempered, helpful, extremely considerate. He literally smothers me with his love. He has no other interest in life but me, and his entire world revolves around me, my interests, my friends and hobbies. No amount of encouraging has ever been able to convince him to develop interests of his own. I wish I could love him the way he loves me. But, you see, I also have a lover . . ."

When the court nonetheless awarded her a divorce, his home, his children, and substantial alimony—allowing him only once-a-month visitation rights—Mr. Merry entirely lost his grasp on the real world, and after he threatened to kill his wife, a judge committed him permanently to our clinic on the petition, of course, of his ex-wife.

We were forced to lock Mr. Merry up in a padded cell. At night, the attendants reported, they could hear him howling rather like a wolf, cursing and reciting in a disjointed manner what appeared to be fragments of Holy Scripture, punctuated with shouts and imprecations. Monitoring his insane monologue, we soon discerned that the passages were from Mary Baker Eddy's *Science and Health with Key to the Scriptures*:

". . . Civil Law, I say, establishes very unfair differences between the rights of the two sexes.#&$*(%(! Christian Science furnishes no precedent for such #*$(%¢($ injustice, and civilization mitigates it in some measure . . . @#($*%¢#*¢! Our laws are not impartial, to say the least, in their discrimination as to the person, property, and parental claims of the two sexes. @#&$&%#*%! If the elective franchise for women will remedy the evil without encouraging difficulties of greater magnitude, let us hope it will be granted . . . @#¢$&%*! Want of uniform justice is a crying evil caused by the selfishness and inhumanity of man . . . @#¢$*$(%! Divorces should warn the age of some fundamental error in the marriage state. The union of the sexes suffers fearful discord . . . @#$&#*$($*%(¢!"

The Confessions of a Former Feminist

Not long ago, a male sympathizer in Florida sent us a recording of a remarkable speech by a seventy-year-old woman to a group of churchwomen. The woman said she had "humiliated three fine husbands" and advised the ladies to marry a man who won't put up with any nonsense from them. Surprisingly, she was roundly applauded.

Not surprisingly, however, this extraordinary speech went unreported in the nation's press. In it, the woman declared that "everything that any woman has ever done wrong I did first." She confessed to having been an adulterous drunk. She also said she had treated her three husbands like toys and her son ended up on skid row. This, she said, "was another of my many responsibilities in ruining men."

"By and large," she said, "American women aren't happy . . . We are all the time trying to win, but with us women, it's the winners who lose in the end. I know about that. I won time after time over my three husbands, and I ended up in a suicide attempt."

But the woman insisted it's the men's fault. "Most of the problem of our being what we are today is the men's fault. They let us get away with it. If the men would be men, we would not be allowed to get away with the murder we are getting away with. We win because the men allow us to. They get sick and tired of it all and they give up. They are so tired of aggressive, competitive women. An aggressive, competitive woman is against nature, and men everywhere are retreating from her. The man retreats from fatherhood, too, and then we women end up playing the role of father as well as mother, and so both the male child and the female child grow up under petticoat domination.

The woman warned that this is leading many men into homosexuality. "The man can no longer respond sexually to an aggressive woman, and then the woman stands over him and says: 'Can't you even be a man?' " Not far from her home is a Marine base. "You would not believe the young Marines in their early twenties who have sat in my living room and told me that they were impotent in the sex act for this reason." She said that she had once asked a young man, whose problem was homosexuality, why homosexuality was on the increase.

He said, "You women no longer permit us men to cherish you."

"Woman," said the speaker, "has gone around for the past twenty-five years beating her bosom, saying my IQ is as high as your IQ; I have more college degrees than you do. And yet there is an increase in alcoholism among women, in perversion among women, in the use of barbiturates, in divorces, in suicide attempts. If women are so bright, so mentally equipped, so educated that they are superior to men, why is the incidence of failure so high in all the female statistics? Yes, our brains are more educated than they have ever been, and our hearts less so. American women know that they have failed. We know that our home is the most important thing in the world, but somehow we have lost our way."

THE LOCKHORNS

" PLEASE BE MORE EXPLICIT, MADAM....
WHICH DIRTY, ROTTEN, DRUNKEN BUM?"

She said that she had recently talked with an old friend whose marriage had just collapsed and she couldn't understand why. "What," she asked, "if you had cooked his meals with grace? What if you had gone to the door of an evening to greet him with a loving welcome? What if you had been kind to his friends? What if you had listened instead of talked? What if you had never made fun of him, or never interrupted him, or contradicted him, or belittled him and his stories? There wouldn't have been an IQ on earth that could have competed with you."

"Women," concluded this seventy-year-old former feminist, "have gained their rights in this country and have lost their privileges. The greatest job on the face of the earth is one I never did—to be an intelligent, joyous, tender wife, and an intelligent, joyous, tender mother. I never did this. I had three chances at it, and I never did it once. This was the one thing that could have kept me from drunkenness, that could have given me the peace inside which I wanted so badly, that could have brought me to God earlier."

THE LOCKHORNS

"HAVE YOU SEEN THIS LITTLE QUIZ, LORETTA? ACCORDING TO THIS OUR MARRIAGE IS A COMPLETE FAILURE!"

Behind
Every Great Madman
Is a Woman

In pursuit of further evidence to support the self-evident truth of Samra's Law, Professor Kapliwatsky and I and our able staff also conducted extensive research into the lives of the five hundred most eminent men of the past century— philosophers, scientists, playwrights, novelists, poets, actors, dancers, statesmen, politicians. This research was, of course, laborious and consumed many years. But we persisted, examining their biographies and autobiographies, interviewing thousands of persons who had known them, and letting no detail escape our attention.

We confined our study to the great men of the nineteenth and twentieth centuries because these were the centuries which were most influenced by the feminist movement. We were, of course, unable to use controls, but our methods were impeccable. I am happy to report that we are now able to tell the results of our research.

THE LOCKHORNS

"STRANGE. THEY HAVE A NEW BOOK ON MARITAL HAPPINESS LISTED UNDER SCIENCE FICTION."

Without exception, we found that every last man of our great men had had troubles with a wife, wives, mothers, lady friends, mistresses, barmaids, or all of these. Indeed, the percentage of great men who quarreled regularly with members of the opposite sex far exceeded that of the drunk driver group which we referred to in an earlier chapter.

We also discovered that the problems with women which nagged at these great men throughout their lives were remarkably similar from matriarchy to matriarchy, notwithstanding the variables of culture. For instance, Jean Cocteau in France suffered in much the same way that J. M. Barrie suffered in England and Robert Frost suffered in America. Cocteau's father killed himself when his son was ten, and afterwards Cocteau lived for many years with his mother in Paris apartments. An opium addict for much of his life, Cocteau became a homosexual early in the game and tried hard to preserve his youth with frequent hair dyings and face lifts, according to his biographer Francis Steegmuller.

In England, Barrie was never able to escape from the clutches of his strong-willed and possessive mother. Barrie's biographer, Janet Dunbar, contends that Barrie was permanently crippled by his relationship with his mother, and his marriage to a young actress was never consummated and ended in divorce.

In America, Robert Frost's family life could only be described as hellish. According to Lawrence Thompson, his biographer, Frost's son committed suicide, two of his daughters were divorced, a third daughter suffered from mental illness, and Frost's wife "whose bleak depressions seem scarcely ever to have lifted, died without permitting him access to her deathbed."

Space does not permit us to explore herein the lives of all five hundred of our great men. However, as examples, let us take a representative group—the writers and philosophers. (See Figure 4.)

The male-woman first appeared in the nineteenth century in the West. In Russia she bedeviled Tolstoy, Dostoyevsky, and Chekhov. In Germany she bedeviled Karl Marx, Schopenhauer, and Nietzsche. In Austria, Freud. In Denmark, Kierkegaard. In Sweden, Strindberg. In America, Poe and Mark Twain. In England, John Ruskin.

FIGURE 4

Great Men, Their Mates, and Their Fates

Great Man	Times Married	State of Marriage(s)	Died Young	Died Mad	Died Drunk
Karl Marx	1	Turbulent			X
Leo Tolstoy	1	Turbulent		X	
Arthur Schopenhauer	0			X	
Friedrich Wilhelm Nietzsche	0			X	
Sören Kierkegaard	0		X	X	
Johann August Strindberg	2	Turbulent		X	
Sigmund Freud	1	Unhappy		X	
John Ruskin	1	Never consummated		X	
W. Somerset Maugham	0				
Rupert Brooke	0		X	X	
Trevenen Huxley	0		X		
Oscar Wilde	1	Unhappy	X	X	
Bertrand Russell	4	Turbulent		X	
Ernest Hemingway	4	Turbulent	X	X	
F. Scott Fitzgerald	1	Turbulent	X	X	X
Sherwood Anderson	4	Turbulent			
Eugene O'Neill	3	Turbulent		X	X
John O'Hara	3	Turbulent			X
Hart Crane	0		X		X
John Steinbeck	3	Turbulent			
Sinclair Lewis	2	Turbulent	X	X	X
Westbrook Pegler	3	Turbulent			
James Agee	2	Turbulent	X		
William Faulkner	1	Turbulent			X
William Saroyan	2	Turbulent			
Jean Cocteau	0				
J. M. Barrie	1	Turbulent			
Robert Frost	1	Turbulent			
Henry Miller	5	Turbulent			
J. D. Salinger	2	Turbulent			
Norman Mailer	3	Turbulent			
Saul Bellow	3	Turbulent			
Truman Capote	0				
Edward Albee	0				
Tennessee Williams	0				
Gore Vidal	0				
Allen Ginsberg	0				

In addition to playing the stock market, Karl Marx, the prophet of Communism, did not get on well with his wife, was often brutal to her, drank heavily, and seduced his wife's maid and fathered her child, we are told by no less an authority than Robert Payne. Much of Marx's life was spent in conflict with the opposite sex, and this perhaps more than economics—and perhaps even more than his envious nature—shaped his lust for violence and finally, his call for violent revolution and bloody class conflict.

THE LOCKHORNS

WE'D BETTER STAY HOME. IT'S NOT A FIT NIGHT OUT FOR MAN OR BEAST."

It has been supposed from his writings that Tolstoy's principal battles were with himself as adversary, but Henri Troyat's monumental biography suggests that the Russian novelist's principal adversary was his wife, Sonya, who curiously conceded that she often felt like "a devil near a saint." Tolstoy's endless battles with Sonya are legendary, and on at least two occasions ended in Tolstoy's mental breakdown. Both times he was slow in recovering.

Tolstoy and Sonya each kept a detailed day-to-day diary in which they set down their innermost and most private thoughts, moods, and feelings about the world and about one another. At the end of each day, before retiring, they would exchange diaries, a practice which they persisted in despite the outbreaks of anguish and hysteria that would inevitably follow the reading of them. "The miracle is," says Troyat, "that their marriage stood the strain of this continual rivalry to see which could be most truthful."

"I have a senseless and involuntary desire to test my power over him; that is, I want to make him obey me," Sonya wrote. "It hurts me to look at him or hear him or be near him, as it must hurt a devil to be near a saint."

"I can only say," Tolstoy wrote of his wife, "that her most striking feature is that of a 'man of integrity'—I mean what I say: both 'integrity' and 'man.' . . . I arrive in the morning, full of joy and gladness, and I find the countess in a tantrum; everything collapses, and I stand there as though I had been scalded. I am afraid of everything, and I see that there can be no happiness or poetry for me except when I am alone. I am kissed tenderly, out of habit, but then the quarrels resume immediately . . ."

Troyat observes that when war with Poland threatened, "the fact was that he [Tolstoy] wanted to enlist less to exterminate the Poles than to get away from his wife."

Tolstoy's disciple Chertkov also often quarreled with Sonya. "If I had a wife like you," Chertkov was to tell Sonya, "I would have blown my brains out long ago, or gone to America." Tolstoy almost did.

For Tolstoy, a woman lost her best qualities the moment she left the home. "When religious feeling wanes in a society, it means that woman's power is waxing," he wrote later in life, in a fit of despair.

Schopenhauer was a confirmed bachelor and woman hater. His mother, a widow, has been described by one biographer as "smug, castrating, and competitive with her son." He once pushed her down a flight of stairs. Schopenhauer was clearly paranoid, lived in terror of assassination and robbery, and in his later years, slept with an arsenal of guns and knives tucked under his pillow.

Nietzsche, another angry bachelor, had perhaps more than his share of problems with the emerging feminists of his times. Perhaps it is no coincidence the German philosopher concluded that "God is dead" at the precise time that the feminists began to march. Nietzsche mounted a systematic attack on religion without, however, ever realizing that it was the feminists, and not himself nor churchmen, who were finally to kill God. If God were indeed dead, the goddesses were very much alive and kicking, and most of the ones of Nietzsche's time survived him. Nietzsche's obsession with "the will to power" and the "superman" is merely an implicit admission that he, and indeed all men, had lost that power which had begun to pass to the feminists. Nietzsche's writings were later to inspire the Nazis, which should not surprise the reader, knowing now what he does of Samra's Law. He lived out the last ten years of his life in a mental institution, an incurable schizophrenic, more dead than God, less powerful than the staff matrons who bathed, clothed, fed him, and put him to bed.

"What is woman for man? A dangerous toy," Nietzsche declared. And he blamed Ibsen, whom he called "that typical old maid," for creating "the emancipated woman." Nietzsche contended that democracy and feminism leveled everybody, making women of men and men of women. "Here is little of man; therefore women try to make themselves manly." He believed that no society could achieve equality of the sexes because war between the sexes is eternal, and peace comes only when one or the other is acknowledged master.

And then Nietzsche, in calling for the superman (when perhaps he is actually calling for men to stand up and be men), declares: "For only he who is enough of a man will save the woman in woman."

THE LOCKHORNS

"DID IT EVER OCCUR TO YOU THAT MAYBE I DON'T **WANT** TO COMMUNICATE WITH YOU?"

Kierkegaard, the melancholy Dane, lost his nerve as his wedding to his beloved Regina approached, and then abruptly broke the engagement. He remained a bachelor to the end of his short life, unable to summon the courage to marry. Kierkegaard, too, suffered attacks of madness during these difficult times, and his writings, besides displaying a great religiosity, were filled with lamentations over his lack of courage and loss of Regina.

Strindberg, a chronic misogynist, had an obsessive distrust of women. Women, he once said, "admire swindlers, quack dentists, braggadocios of literature, peddlers of wooden spoons—everything mediocre." He was insanely jealous of his second wife's attentions to other men. Two of his marriages failed, and he too went mad and spent the last years of his life in an institution.

Freud was not the product of a happy family. His father was a weak man who deferred both to his wife's and his son's opinions. Later the founder of psychoanalysis was to discover that most of his patients were victims of family strife, and Freud spent the rest of his days analyzing interminably their relationships with their fathers, mothers, and spouses. Indeed psychoanalysis was born in the wake of the feminist movement. Freud and his disciples were to reap a harvest of madmen, homosexuals, women haters, male-women, alcoholics, et al., from the seeds sown by the early feminists, including, I might add, Mary Baker Eddy. Even Freud's theories of female "penis envy" and male "castration complexes" were merely acknowledgments of the rise of the male-woman. Freud provided some rather insightful analyses of the problem, but no solutions, though he did hint at one when he observed—in an echo of Tolstoy—that madness became epidemic in modern times with the decline of religion. In the past, men of good will had relied upon religion to save them from the bitch and the witch. Now there was nothing but psychiatry, but it became increasingly clear to many men in the twentieth century that neither psychoanalysis nor chemotherapy nor vitamins could save them from a nagging wife or a Woman's Liberationist.

In all of Freud's works, there are hundreds of disparaging references to women. "The great question that has never been answered and which I have not yet been able to answer, despite my thirty years of research into the feminine soul, is

'What does a woman want?' " Women likewise confounded Freud's disciples. Another early psychoanalyst, Wilhelm Stekel, wrote, "I have found among many women an imperative need to humiliate their men; I may say that this is the rule in marriage."

In England, John Ruskin was also having his problems. In the *Letters of John Ruskin to Lord and Lady Mount-Temple*, we are told, "when his mother was nearly ninety and Ruskin fifty-two, she still ruled her son and her household with inexorable kindness." Ruskin's marriage to Effie Gray was never consummated. It was finally annulled "by reason of Ruskin's incurable impotency." Ruskin suffered a series of mental breakdowns and was insane the last ten years of his life.

Somerset Maugham's homosexuality was well known, and at his death *The Times* noted, in a bit of an understatement, that he had "a certain waspishness for women." (I met him on a boat in Alexandria in 1955, and he had not lost that waspishness.) He was said to have had one great love in his life. According to a publisher who was interviewed at his death, "She was Rosie, you know, Rosie, the barmaid in *Cakes and Ale*. There's also someone like her near the end of *Of Human Bondage*. I don't know who she was, but she did exist. Whatever happened, I don't know. But after that he never cared tuppence for another woman."

Rupert Brooke, the English poet, cracked up as the result of complications over a love affair. Trevenen Huxley, brother to Aldous and Julian, hung himself after an unhappy romance. After an unhappy marriage, Oscar Wilde could resist everything but homosexuality. Dylan Thomas and Brendan Behan drenched themselves in alcohol and died early deaths after a series of turbulent romances.

Bertrand Russel's four marriages were so successful as to

lead him to propose trial marriage. The great man was like putty in the hands of at least a couple of his wives, two of whom were Americans. In *The Autobiography of Bertrand Russell*, we find Lord Russell referring to his third wife, the brilliant and beautiful Patricia Spence, as "Peter." "When Peter left me . . ." he writes. Sidney Hook notes that Patricia Spence, or Peter, "was almost forty years his junior, and he doted on her in an obvious and pathetic way. Her leaving him was one of the most shattering experiences in his life. His grief was compounded by her refusal to let him see his son, Conrad, to whom he was profoundly devoted. The wound was so deep that it probably explains the almost total black-out of their courtship, their life in America, her role in the imbroglio with Albert C. Barnes that contributed to permanently embittering his feelings about America, and the events leading to her desertion."

Hook also points out that "Russell always regarded his daughter Kate, by his second marriage, as intellectually close to him, as one who shared his views. She was reared without a shred of religious education in the best militant secular tradition. Here she suddenly turns up a fanatical Christian missionary with a parson for a husband! There is no elaboration or explanation of this unexpected conversion. One wonders whether this incident led Russell to any second thoughts about the validity of his earlier views on child rearing and religious education."

But the male-woman had perhaps her most devastating impact in the twentieth century on writers in America, where it all began. Her influence on art was immeasurable, as all at once American writers became obsessed with the same themes: broken romances, crumbling marriages, homosexuality, violence, death.

Hemingway had four marriages, and this fact perhaps more

than anything else may explain why all his life he was obsessed with violence and death. His father shot himself in 1928. A. E. Hotchner recalls that one night Hemingway had been drinking and "he called to me and came down the hall. 'What you should know, because we level with each other,' he said, 'is what my mother said that time I went back for my inheritance. 'Don't disobey me,' she said, 'or you'll regret it all your life as your father did.' "

Several years later, at Christmastime, Hemingway received a package from his mother containing the revolver with which his father had killed himself. The card simply said that she thought he might like to have it. Hemingway was to confess to Hotchner: "I spend a hell of a lot of time killing animals and fish so I won't kill myself."

Scott Fitzgerald married the first of the flappers, and the first of the flappers died mad. Zelda Fitzgerald, writes Nancy Milford in her biography, *Zelda*, "was the American Girl living the American Dream, and she became mad within it." Zelda suffered a series of mental breakdowns, was pronounced an incurable schizophrenic, and was continually in and out of sanitariums and institutions the rest of her life. Beautiful, brilliant, talented, Zelda was put on a pedestal from the outset by her husband; she became the golden girl of his novels and stories. The Fitzgeralds lived fast, drank hard, fought furiously, slept around, and in the end, drove one another up the walls. Hemingway knew them, and understood that Zelda was jealous of her husband's work. Fitzgerald was so cowed by this madwoman that he even accepted Zelda's taunts about his sexual prowess. "This was a time," Fitzgerald wrote, when "a widespread neurosis began to be evident," and many of his contemporaries "had begun to disappear into the dark maw of violence." Fitzgerald himself was soon to disappear into the dark maw of alcoholism. He died young, as so many American men do, of a heart attack. Zelda's looks, meantime, faded early and her skin took on the yellowish hue of the schizophrenic. Curiously, in her later years she became known for her bizarre religiosity.

Sherwood Anderson had four wives, none of whom appeared to please him greatly. His third wife, Elizabeth Prall Anderson, has just written her memoirs. The depth of Anderson's affection for Elizabeth is suggested in a letter he wrote to her when she was vacationing in California in 1929. "I just wish you would not come back," he wrote. She didn't.

THE LOCKHORNS

"I'LL **BET** YOU'VE BEEN BUSY AS A BEE ....MAKING A LITTLE HONEY, RIGHT?"

Eugene O'Neill's relationship with his second wife, the writer Agnes Boulton, was "scarred by constant fighting, jealous quarrels and reconciliations." They were ideally unsuited to one another. O'Neill was married three times in all, enough to explain the suffocating depression, violence, madness, drinking and long-windedness that haunt his plays. An alcoholic, he finally died of a disease of the brain.

John O'Hara was also married three times. His first marriage ended after two years. O'Hara had bad teeth, bad nerves, a bad stomach, and drank in heroic proportions.

Hart Crane was a child of family strife. "I think it's time you realized," he wrote his mother when he was twenty, "that for the last eight years my youth has been a rather bloody battleground for your's and father's sex life and troubles." His mother was variously described by biographer John Unterecker as greedy, hysterical, cannibalistic, possessive, and self-righteous—a nervous case given to hatreds, scenes, dramas, demands, recriminations, accusations, and withdrawals. His businessman father was described as weak and uncomprehending. His parents were later divorced. Crane became famous for his drinking bouts and his trips to the waterfront to pick up sailors. In 1931 he established a heterosexual relationship for the first time with an attractive, intellectual woman, who, like his mother, was also a nervous case. He and the woman planned to get married and took a boat trip together. In Havana they quarreled. Crane got drunk and, after a wild night, told the woman, "I'm not going to make it, dear. I'm utterly disgraced." He then threw himself overboard. Age, thirty-three.

John Steinbeck lasted through three marriages. And while Hemingway's and Fitzgerald's marriages drove them to alcohol, Steinbeck merely took to traveling. Traveling became a way of life for him. He was forever on the move. And his trips so annoyed one of his wives that she sued for divorce, receiving a $220,000 settlement.

In his biography of Sinclair Lewis, Mark Schorer tells us a

great deal about Lewis' stormy marriages, first to a young woman with elegant manner and accent, and then to a high-powered journalist, Dorothy Thompson. Dorothy Thompson, Schorer declares, "struggled to preserve an intense but embittered marriage, trying to understand Lewis' mixture of furious envy and admiration. (If Dorothy became President, he said, he would write a column called 'My Day.') But everything went smash and for Lewis nothing remained but loneliness, frantic motion and death." Much of the time, the author of *Babbitt* was drunk and shouting, purchasing nostrums to increase his sexual prowess, whipping himself into wild rages, trembling with the dt's.

Westbrook Pegler was married thrice, which may account for the fierce mien that he habitually wore. "For myself," the jaundiced Pegler once remarked, "I will say that my hates always occupied my mind much more actively and have given me greater spiritual satisfaction."

The poet Theodore Roethke had his problems with women, and the novelist James Agee had a couple marriages go bad on him. Agee was rendered so bewildered and grieved over the breakup of his marriages that he died in his prime. Faulkner, like Hemingway, was famous for his epic drinking bouts and his obsession with violence.

Henry Miller, the virtuoso of the bedroom, suffered through five marriages. At one time, after World War II, his French publisher had amassed $40,000 in royalties, but Miller did not go to France to collect the money. "I was having a fight with my wife," he explained, "and I didn't want to take her."

J. D. Salinger's first marriage was to a European woman physician. It didn't work out. Later, he married an English-born Radcliffe student. Salinger threw a party to celebrate his second marriage, which was reportedly attended by his second wife's first husband. He has since withdrawn from public view.

After three marriages (one to a writer, another to a painter, and a third to an actress), Norman Mailer had this to say in *Christians and Cannibals*: "I think the womanization of America comes not only because women are becoming more selfish, more greedy, less romantic, less warm, more lusty, and more filled with hate—but because the men have collaborated with them. There's been a change in the minds of most men about the function of marriage—it isn't that they've necessarily become weaker vis-a-vis their wives, it's that they've married women who will be less good for them in the home and more good for them in the world." Mailer, too, became obsessed with violence and homosexuality. ("Girl, if you was a boy and I was queer I could go for you," he wrote in *The Village Voice* some time ago.) He was once hospitalized after stabbing one of his wives during a quarrel. In middle age, Mailer took up boxing.

Saul Bellow has had three marriages, a son by each wife, and three divorces. Not much more successful with the male-woman were Truman Capote, Edward Albee, Tennessee Williams, Gore Vidal, or Allen Ginsberg. The frequency with which the themes of homosexuality and violence recur together in American literature suggests some kind of re-lationship, does it not? Professor Kapliwatsky thinks so.

"I am a definition of hysteria," admits Tennessee Williams, a hypochondriac who says he sometimes lives on drink and pills. His father, C. C. Williams, a shoe salesman, had been happiest "playing poker with men and drinking." On those few occasions when his father was home, Williams recalls that his parents often "quarreled horribly." He came close to marriage only once, as a teenager. But he had a nervous breakdown.

Gore Vidal's mother, Nina Gore, was, according to her son, "a real flapper of the twenties," beautiful, a Washington belle. "We haven't spoken in years," says Vidal. She divorced Eugene Vidal and married Hugh D. Auchincloss, who later became husband to the mother of Jackie Kennedy Onassis. Of *Myra Breckinridge*, Vidal says: "There's an uneasy masculinity in my country, and it was a fascinating literary task to write about castration and being buggered, every man's fear . . . Modern American writers are preoccupied by the 'castrating U.S. woman.' In print, they pay off women for some grudge in their own psyches or treat them as pneumatic mattresses for their lust . . ."

Will anyone ever forget William Saroyan's public confession in the *Saturday Evening Post* several years ago? The Armenian-American author gloomily described his marriage to an emancipated woman and how he had divorced her once and remarried her again after a valiant attempt at reconciliation, only to divorce her a second time in a final admission of defeat. The Orientals, Saroyan concluded, may have been right about women after all.

The really rare American writer is one like Harding (Pete) Lemay, the playwright, whose remarkable autobiography *Inside, Looking Out*, is a hymn of praise to his second wife. Lemay had a turbulent family life on a farm in Canada. His father was a suicide, his mother had a mental breakdown, and his first marriage to an actress ended in disaster. In his second wife, Dorothy Shaw, and his in-laws, Lemay found the things "that make life make sense to men." Of his in-laws he says, "Within their presence, I slowly became a son, as in the company of their daughter I became a man." Lemay looks upon his second marriage as "my great good fortune" and as his "only anchor in an insane world."

It is clear that the wisest and the most courageous of us, the brightest and the most talented, did not fare so well in our dealings with the male-woman of this century. But then, the feminists, in many respects, did not do so well either. Much is said of the successes of the "new woman," but we rarely hear of her defeats: Zelda's madness, Betty Friedan's divorce, Marilyn Monroe's suicide, Marie MacDonald's suicide, Virginia Woolf's suicide after a series of mental breakdowns, Grace Metalious' death from a chronic liver ailment, Dorothy Kilgallen's death from an overdose of alcohol and barbiturates, Clara Bow's nervous disorders and recurrent trips to sanitariums; Pamela Moore's blowing her brains out, Janice Joplin's death from an overdose of drugs. . . . A group of California psychiatrists recently discovered that most of the wrist slashers admitted to one mental hospital were bright, talented, college-educated women.

America's writers have merely reflected, in their lives as well as in their work, the madness of our times, an era that has witnessed a seemingly inexhaustible parade of women haters march into the news.

THE LOCKHORNS

"IF YOU'VE ALREADY GIVEN ME THE BEST YEARS OF YOUR LIFE, THEN I HAVE NOTHING TO LOOK FORWARD TO, HAVE I ?"

© King Features Syndicate, Inc., 1968. World rights reserved

Women and Violence,
Women and War
(Oh, Woman,
Thy Name Is Frailty?)

Women have always had a special talent for bringing down the strong and the powerful. Delilah's treachery finished off Samson. In Greek mythology, Hercules was driven mad by his wife and slew her and his children.

It is perhaps no coincidence that the Romans personified the moon as a goddess and called her Luna. In those times in Rome, as in India, it was commonly believed that when the moon was full, all kinds of demons and witches came out in force. Men went mad and were driven to crimes of violence when Luna was in her full glory. Others were transformed into wolf-men. Even today police officers have noted the increase in the incidence of crimes of violence when the moon is full. Thus we owe the term "lunatic" to a goddess.

The ancient feminist Margaret Mead recently warned neo-feminists that "Women's Liberation has to be terribly conscious about the danger of provoking men to kill women. You have quite literally driven them mad." This is the same woman who predicts that a switch in sexual roles is in the offing and "men may actually discover they want to stay home to mind the children now."

THE LOCKHORNS

"I WANT TO ENROLL IN THE SAME COURSE MY WIFE TOOK!"

Women are still driving men to murder. William Manchester, in his book *The Death of a President*, says that Lee Harvey Oswald "was going mad" at the time he assassinated John F. Kennedy, and that the catalyst for Oswald's madness was his destructive relationship with his wife, Marina. Oswald supposed that he had found a "beautiful, dedicated Communist" when he married Marina, but instead, says Manchester, he had found a scold.

Oswald's wife hounded and jeered at him. "There were many fights, and Marina, a quick girl with a knee, was the better fighter." Oswald cringed, wept, and fell to his knees "as the great darkness of his private nightmare enveloped him." Not long before the assassination, Marina left Oswald and moved herself and her daughter into the home of a friend. (Oswald's own parents had been divorced.)

What did John F. Kennedy share in common with his assassin? A troubled marriage.

John Kennedy's health was never good, but marriage did not improve it. Kennedy, according to his confidant Ted Sorenson, suffered "from a multitude of physical ailments. He used and carried with him about the country more pills, potions, poultices, and other paraphernalia than would be found in a small dispensary. As a Congressman, he was so pale and thin that his colleagues feared for his life. His stomach was always sensitive . . ."

"There are two kinds of women," Jacqueline Kennedy once said, "those who want power in the world and those who want power in bed." Jackie's colossal egocentricity was not likely to have endeared her to the President over the long pull. According to Susan Sheehan, writing in *The New York Times Magazine*, a friend of Jackie's once asked her if she'd recently seen a tiny, gay interior decorator who had been helping her embellish her New York apartment. "Oh yes," Jackie answered, "I did see him the other day. I almost stepped on him in the elevator."

In her book *My Boss, Jackie Kennedy*, Mary B. Gallagher tells us, in a single passage, a good deal about a marriage which the public supposed was ideal: "I sometimes thought it would be nice if Jackie would eat breakfast with the Senator —or at least come downstairs to see him off . . . I always felt that there were two things that John F. Kennedy wanted in his home: a comfortable, familiar, unchanging place to read in peace and quiet—and no money worries. Strangely enough, these two things remained elusive."

President Kennedy's strained relations with his wife may or may not have had something to do with the fact that, under his administration, the United States lost its cool and waged an abortive invasion of Cuba and got into a discouraging and bloody land war in Vietnam. Both mistakes might have been avoided if cooler tempers had prevailed in the White House and Jackie had eaten breakfast with the President.

Richard Nixon, like St. Francis and Mohammed, recognized the limitless capacity of women to make trouble. In his book *The Resurrection of Richard Nixon*, Jules Witcover reports that President Nixon made the following comment about American women in an interview several years ago:

"They're the real haters. Any Machiavellian scheme, they go for. They die hard. They tell me, 'You didn't hit them hard enough. Why don't you give them hell like Truman?' I explain I not only have to appeal to partisan Republicans but also have to get Democrats to cross over. But the women don't understand that. Occasionally I say a good word for Johnson or Humphrey. It's a device, of course, to show I'm fair-minded, but the women don't see that. That's why the women liked Barry so. He didn't give a damn about the Democrats."

American presidents have, with few exceptions, been notorious for their lack of taste in women. Lincoln's wife was a millstone around his neck, and a divided, Civil War-wracked nation was merely a reflection of the divisions in the White House. In his recent book *Roosevelt: The Soldier of Freedom*, James MacGregor Burns emphasizes the physical and temperamental isolation of Eleanor Roosevelt from the President. He also recalls her surprise and anguish upon learning, after her husband's death, that he had been seeing Lucy Mercer Rutherford.

Women drive men to suicide. A highly placed official of a major college recently killed himself because of marital troubles.

Women drive men up towers. Not long ago, Kenneth Boyle, twenty-eight, of Jersey City, New Jersey, was driving across the George Washington Bridge when he stopped his car, got out and climbed a 650-foot tower. Both his wife and his mother-in-law were in the car and they had all been quarreling. "You go your way, and I'll go mine," he shouted, before police finally subdued him and took him to a hospital for observation.

Women drive men to violence. In America today, even our peace movements are violent. The FBI recently arrested Angela Davis, charged with collaboration in the murder of California Judge Harold J. Haley, who was kidnapped by three men from a courtroom. The shotgun that killed Judge Haley had been bought by Miss Davis, the former UCLA philosophy instructor and self-professed Communist. ("You've got it all, African woman. You're the most powerful stimulus I have," wrote George Jackson, a black militant accused of murder, to Angela Davis from his cell in California's Soledad Prison.) On July 17, 1970, after he was served with divorce papers, Jim Dearman of Brooksville, Florida, suddenly went berserk. He went looking for his wife with a pistol, but instead killed an innocent bystander. Dearman died in a hail of police bullets. In Brighton, Massachusetts on September 26, 1970, three men and two women, with guns blazing, robbed the Boston State Street Bank and Trust Company of $26,000 in cash and, while making their getaway, killed a patrolman. The FBI started a nationwide hunt for the five, and found the three men but still haven't located the two women, Katherine Power and Susan Saxe. Both coeds are members of the Women's Liberation Movement. Forcible rapes, meantime, have increased 116 percent in the past decade, according to the FBI.

Betty Friedan, the mother hen of the Women's Liberation Movement, was the daughter of a woman who "belittled, cut down my father because she had no place to channel her terrific energies." In turn, her marriage to Carl Friedan, an advertising executive, was stormy. "When they went out socially," writes Paul Wilkes in *The New York Times*, "the Friedans would as often fight as not." The success of her book *The Feminine Mystique*, reports Wilkes, "brought her grief in private life. 'I probably appeared on more talk shows with black eyes than without,' she says. 'Carl hated my success and he would throw my schedules, my notes all over the house.'

In Detroit, a former University of Michigan All-American football star, Bill Yearby, was charged with assault with intent to commit murder in the stabbing of his estranged wife. Police said that Yearby, ordinarily an easy-going fellow, went wild when his wife, awaiting a final divorce decree, refused to allow him to take his 1½-year-old daughter for a short visit. His mother-in-law told police the couple had quarreled violently ever since their marriage four years ago.

In Los Angeles, television sportscaster Stan Duke was convicted of second-degree murder in the February 7, 1971 slaying of radio commentator Averill Berman. Duke's lawyers contended that the KNXT sports reporter had "blacked out" after seeing his estranged wife engaged in a sex act with Berman.

In Grand Rapids, Michigan, on May 10, 1971, Union High School was closed indefinitely in the wake of brawling between white and black students. Principal Thomas Neat said that the trouble had been building for about two weeks, and that there had been several fights earlier, always involving girls. He reported that girls appeared to trigger the previous day's fighting with volleys of racial insults.

Women make delinquents of men's children. Judge Samuel S. Leibowitz, senior judge of Brooklyn's highest criminal court, visited Italy not long ago to find out why it has the lowest juvenile delinquency rate of any Western country. Reported Judge Leibowitz: "Every criminal courts judge in this country is sickeningly aware of the terrible fact that teenagers are replacing adults on the criminal dockets. What Western country has the lowest juvenile delinquency rate? The answer is Italy . . . I went into Italian homes to see for myself. I found that even in the poorest family the father is respected by the wife and children as its head. He rules with varying degrees of love and tenderness and firmness. His household has rules to live by, and the child who disobeys them is punished. Thus I found the nine-word principle that I think can do more for us than all the committees, ordinances, and multimillion-dollar programs combined: *Put Father back at the head of the family.* The American teenager has been raised in a household where 'obey' is an outlawed word, and where the mother has put herself at the head of the family. Every time Mother overrules Father, undermining his authority and standing in the child's eyes [sic], she knocks a piece off the foundation on which the child stands."

James W. Stennis, a black man who is the director of the Maxey Boys Training School in Whitmore Lake, Michigan, recently reported that in a study conducted at the institution for delinquent youths, the characteristics of the boys' backgrounds included an "absence of stable father figure at home" and "mother was the dominant parental figure in the home."

"If Charles wanted anything, I'd give it to him," the mother of Charles Manson told a reporter after Manson was convicted in the Sharon Tate murder trial. "Everything was just handed to him, I admit. He never had to do a thing to earn what he wanted. He didn't even have to do things around the house, like rake leaves or mow lawns." Manson was born out of wedlock and never knew his father. He himself married in 1955, fathered a son, and was divorced while serving time in prison.

THE LOCKHORNS

"LOOK, YOU'RE ALWAYS COMPLAINING ABOUT NOT DOING THINGS TOGETHER ···."

When a woman wrote to Billy Graham, disturbed because her "six-year-old son is almost incorrigible—he steals and breaks neighbor children's toys, talks back and is destructive," the evangelist's answer was to the point: "When both parents work, invariably problems develop with the children."

Women cause men who are friends to fight among themselves. New York Rangers goaltender Terry Sawchuk recently died of injuries allegedly received in a fight with his team-mate and friend Ron Stewart. A close friend of Sawchuk told police that Sawchuk had just returned from a futile attempt to reconcile with his wife and was "in a horrible state—beside himself."

Women drive men into early graves. A typical eulogy in a typical metropolitan newspaper obituary: "Literally working nights, Sundays, and holidays, Ronald L. Deathdouspart, 46, who died yesterday of a heart attack during a luncheon with his wife, exemplified the virtues of the highly dedicated public official who moved up through the ranks of the government to the position of department head."

Women drive men to war. Admiral Hyman G. Rickover has testified before the Senate's Foreign Relations Committee that Alexander the Great, Hannibal, Julius Caesar, Napoleon, George Washington, John Paul Jones, Stephen Decatur, Ulysses S. Grant, David Farragut, and other great military commanders were mama's boys. They were not close to their fathers, and their mothers were overprotective and domineering. They went to war to prove their manhood, to find on the battlefront what their fathers had been unable to find at home.

According to D. Clayton James, author of *The Years of MacArthur*, General Douglas MacArthur was a mama's boy tied to his mother by "the most enigmatic affinity within the family." His mother "kept his brown hair in long curls and dressed him in skirts until he was about eight years old." She accompanied her son to the Military Academy at West Point, and when MacArthur was asked by another cadet to room with him, he checked out the invitation with his mother before accepting. Even as MacArthur rose in the ranks of the army, his mother, says James, showed excessive "maternal solicitude."

Is it a coincidence that each of the three heads of state and chief protagonists in World War II—Roosevelt, Stalin and Hitler—had a major problem with the woman closest to him?

Hitler, too, was a mama's boy. In his book *Between the White House and the Brown House*, one of Hitler's favorite cronies, Ernst Franz Sedgwick Hanfstaengl, reports Hitler's problem was that he was "a classical example of the Oedipus complex." Hanfstaengl says Hitler "kept a huge picture of his mother in his bedroom at the Reichs chancellery—facing the bed. He was impotent and a sadist." Until the very end, Hitler was a bachelor.

Stalin, ever the paranoid, quarreled continually with his wife, who finally shot herself. In his memoirs, *Khrushchev Remembers*, Khrushchev gives us a chilling glimpse into the state of Stalin's mind: "Stalin's version of vigilance turned our world into an insane asylum in which everyone was encouraged to search for nonexistent facts about everyone else. The irrational policies of a sick man terrorized us all." "All happy families resemble one another," Stalin's daughter Svetlana Alliluyeva tells us, quoting Tolstoy. "Each unhappy family is unhappy in its own way."

And, of course, it appears that all the while, FDR's heart was elsewhere.

Would world history have been different had Roosevelt, Stalin, and Hitler been happily married? Beyond the shadow of a doubt.

("Schools and colleges are all imbued with the idea that it's the man's world that should be studied," says Dr. Benjamin M. Spock. "I think we should say more about the role women play . . . In history, we should emphasize Napoleon's mother as well as Napoleon.")

Not much has changed over the centuries. Not long ago

Huey P. Newton, minister of defense of the Black Panther Party, said this to the Revolutionary Peoples' Constitutional Convention: "We will change this society. We will use whatever means is necessary. We will have our manhood even if we have to level the earth."

The Vietcong army has made great use of the feminine capacity to make trouble. Nguyen Thi Binh, a strong-willed woman who is a top member of the South Vietnam Liberation Army Military Affairs Party Committee, has issued a directive to party committees and commanders at all echelons to "boldly assign women to appropriate combat missions in replacement of the male sex" and "to train female cadre in every technical service." Madame Binh noted that there are already about four thousand female cadre working in various agencies of the Vietcong military staff, "not including an unspecified number of female cadre serving in assault youth groups." But that, she said, isn't enough.

The Palestinians have learned from both the Israelis and the Vietcong how to harness womanpower. The Palestinian movement's most famous hijacker is Leila Khaled. Dr. Yusuf A. Sayigh, a Palestinian educator, hails "the dramatic transformation in the position of women. The sheltered daughters and sisters of yesterday now spend their time side by side with our men, training and fighting."

The Protestants and Catholics of Northern Ireland were getting along rather well before the appearance in 1969 of Bernadette Devlin, the twenty-three-year-old firebrand who stirred up the Londonderry riots. Bernadette, at this writing, was serving a prison sentence for inciting the riots, and a member of Parliament who visited her reported that she is taking crocheting lessons from an obliging murderess. He added that her temper in prison "is much better than it is normally." Watching the King's Own Scottish Borderers battle with women on a Belfast street recently, a sergeant commented: "The women are the worst of the lot. They egg on the men, and that's when the trouble starts."

It should not be forgotten that the most dreaded of the soldiers of the West African Kingdom of Dahomey were the Amazons, the female warriors who thrived on military organization and waged many successful military campaigns before they were disbanded by the French.

It should not be surprising that the battle cry of the Australian Women's Liberation Movement is: Make War, Not Love.

In America, some of the same women who have been in the forefront of the movement for peace in Vietnam (an admirable cause) have turned their own homes into frightful battlegrounds. They demonstrate for peace in Vietnam in the streets while waging war at home on their husbands, boyfriends, bosses, and sons.

Violence, meantime, is fast reaching epidemic proportions throughout the world, growing apace with women's rights movements. The American Psychiatric Association, viewing the growth of violence as a matter of "urgent concern" for the whole world, plans to dedicate a year of study to the phenomenon. Terrorism, sabotage, rebellion, sedition, rioting, murder, and assassination prevail everywhere, under *all political* and *economic* systems, it has been found.

But violence appears to be especially widespread in America, where, curiously, the feminists have made their greatest gains. The National Commission on the Causes and Prevention of Violence recently concluded that "the 1960s rank as one of our most violent eras, and several of the forms that recent violence has taken are essentially unprecedented in our history . . . In numbers of political assassinations, riots, politically relevant armed group attacks, and demonstrations, the United States since 1948 has been among the half-dozen most tumultuous nations in the world . . . In total magnitude of strife, the United States ranks first among the seventeen Western democracies . . ."

What remains to be explained, the commission declared, is why violence persists in the United States while it has diminished in other countries. This intriguing question remained unanswered until our Society, as we noted earlier, made a study of the 150 most violent men of our times—tyrants, revolutionaries, and assassins—and discovered that the great majority of them were confirmed women haters. In a parallel study, Dr. Fred B. Charatan found that all seven of a group of assassins and would-be assassins of U.S. presidents lacked fathers because of the father's death, divorce, or work schedule. Many of them had been raised by domineering mothers.

Oswald quarreled almost continually with his emancipated Russian wife. Sirhan Sirhan, who assassinated Robert Kennedy, was also a bachelor and the product of a broken home. His parents had had frequent and bitter fights before the father finally divorced the mother and returned to Jordan.

James Earl Ray, who shot Martin Luther King, was also a loner.

George Lincoln Rockwell, the founder of the American Nazi Party, was married and divorced twice. He was a violent, insecure man with lots of hatreds, but with a special hatred for "the queers."

Che Guevara's parents' marriage broke up when he was a boy. Che married Dr. Ilda Gadea, a Peruvian leftist now living in Lima. They were subsequently divorced, and Che married again in Cuba in 1959. Not long afterwards he disappeared and turned up in Bolivia, fighting another guerilla war. He left his second wife in Cuba. Ostensibly he had gone to Bolivia to fight Yankee imperialism, rather than merely to get away from his scond wife. But presuming, for a moment, that he had been born in Miami and suffered through two marriages in the States, it is not unlikely that one day we would have seen him running off to Cuba to fight the Communists.

THE LOCKHORNS

"YOU'RE LEAVING THIS HOUSE OVER MY DEAD BODY!"

4-1

Dr. Charles Wahl, associate professor of psychiatry at the University of California at Los Angeles, has been studying the revolutionary personality since the 1950s, and he concludes that the perpetrators of recent bombings are the neurotic products of unhappy childhoods. "The revolutionary," he observes, "is really reacting to his childhood. If the father was cold, cruel, unloving, and weak, the revolutionary later projects his feelings about his father, or his mother, against organization, against his boss, capitalism, the establishment . . . All the revolutionaries I've seen have almost always experienced a chronic failure in something—work, school, sex. Most persons think that a revolution is motivated by social and economic goals. But that's just not true. The revolutionary is raised at his mother's knee."

Dr. Ames Robey, director of the state of Michigan's Center for Forensic Psychiatry, tells us that most of the insane criminals referred to the Center by the courts have backgrounds of broken homes. Dr. Robey, formerly medical director at Bridgewater State Hospital in Massachusetts, knew Albert DeSalvo, the man who confessed and later denied being the Boston Strangler, and testified at his trial. ("The Boston Strangler," says Robey, "had a violent hatred of women." But he still has doubts that DeSalvo was the Strangler.)

It was a strange temporal coincidence, but Dr. Robey was in Bridgewater, Massachusetts, from 1963 to 1966, when the Boston Strangler was running wild, and not long after he moved to Michigan to assume his new position, there was another outbreak of serial murders—the Ann Arbor coed slayings.

About the same time, Charles Whitman, the Texas tower sniper, went berserk and shot fourteen persons and his wife and mother; Richard Speck, a divorced alcoholic, was murdering eight nurses in Chicago; and the loner William Hollenbaugh was kidnapping Peggy Ann Bradnick in McConnelsburg, Pennsylvania; and in Charleston, West Virginia, two former mental patients killed their mothers.

In New York, Eugene Everett, who had been quarreling with his wife and was enraged with jealousy, shot her and then set fire to her apartment, killing four persons. In St. Cloud, Minnesota, farmer David Hoskins, a church deacon and gospel singer, admitted shooting his wife and then setting fire to his home. His wife and four children died in the fire. In Washington, Thomas Edward Saul, a twenty-seven-year-old mailman being tried for the strangulation-slaying of an eight-year-old girl, testified before a packed courtroom: "All the way back, I always resented women. I just wanted to harm, injure or kill them."

In Albany, New York, Joseph W. White, twenty-five, a state labor department employee, reported for work as usual, pulled a rifle from a box, killed four women employees, and then took his own life. In Ann Arbor, John Burns, a sixty-two-year-old health buff, was sought by police in the killing of a divorcée with a shotgun. The victim, Mrs. Eleanor Farver, had told Burns she didn't want to see him anymore. Mrs. Farver's divorced husband is currently serving a prison term on a charge of burning down her home.

In Hamden, Connecticut, terrified parents kept their children indoors and watched them closely after seven children were found murdered within a period of sixteen months. All of the young victims were girls, and the police were convinced that a madman was on the loose. And in Flint, Michigan, an eighteen-year-old former mental patient confessed to police that he had killed a Wayne State University art instructor, a young woman.

It is Dr. Robey's awesome responsibility to decide for the state of Michigan if a man is sane enough to stand trial. On the day we saw him, Dr. Robey had been called in to evaluate the sanity of a man charged with breaking and entering the home of his divorced wife and chasing her "with intent to do bodily injury less than murder." A couple of years earlier, following a similar assault, he had been committed to a state hospital for the criminally insane as a paranoid schizophrenic. The man was recommitted.

Another case Dr. Robey was evaluating was that of "a seventeen-year-old boy, a wispy, lispy, effeminate boy, who dressed up in his mother's clothes, held up a store, and beat up the woman proprietor. Psychiatrically, he was the victim of a bad mother—a very masculine woman who works in a factory while the boy keeps house."

We asked Dr. Robey what there is about American society that encourages these kinds of crimes—wife murdering, mother killing, coed strangling, murder-suicides, et al.—and whether he thought they are on the increase.

"I don't know," he said, "but all you have to do is read the newspapers, and these things are going on all the time. The Specks. The Whitmans. But offhand the only serial murders I can name that happened in another country were the ones committed by Jack the Ripper."

THE LOCKHORNS

"MY MARRIAGE READS LIKE A FAIRY TALE, EXCEPT THAT I SLEW THE MAIDEN AND MARRIED THE DRAGON."

If American women have a great deal to fear from American men, American men have, perhaps, as much to fear from

American women. Criminologist Leonard Gribble has just written a book called *Such Women Are Deadly*, in which he describes twelve cases of murder by the gentle sex which "will make your skin crawl—each supporting the theory that the female of the species is infinitely more deadly than the male." As if to underscore Gribble's theory, Edith deRham has authored a book called *How Could She Do That: A Study of the Female Criminal*. Observes Miss deRham: "Since women have begun to fight for and gain equal status with men, it was only a question of when—not whether—a woman would make the Ten Most Wanted list . . . With complete equality, we can expect to find more and more women going into hard crime as a means to an end."

Mrs. Paula Newburg, an American criminologist, believes that criminality in women is related to their rights in society. She notes that in such countries as Japan, where women are still relatively protected, female criminal involvement is low. But in America, while women in the past were charged primarily with misdemeanors such as prostitution or drunkenness, today women commit more "male crimes" such as embezzlement and theft, according to Mrs. Newburg.

The most recent FBI figures show that the female crime rate for most offenses is rising faster than the male rate. From 1960 to 1969, male arrests for major crimes rose 61.3 percent; but for females, the increase was 156.2 percent. Los Angeles County Sheriff Peter Pitchess called the increase "startling," and attributed it to the fact that women were "emerging from their traditional roles as housewife and mother."

Boston Juvenile Court Judge Francis G. Poitrast reported that, whereas he once saw ten boys in his courtroom for every girl, now the ratio is three to one.

In Erie, Pennsylvania, Mrs. Peggy Sundberg, a divorcée and former reporter for the *Erie News*, was sentenced to seven to fifteen years in Muncy State Prison for Women for the fatal shooting of her boyfriend.

In Ann Arbor, James Meyers complained to sheriff's deputies that, while he was stopped in traffic, a woman got out of her car and hit him over the head with a tire iron after he became involved in an argument with her male companion, the driver of the car. Meyers was hospitalized.

After Diana Oughton died on March 6, 1970, in a dynamite explosion that demolished a fashionable New York town house, two United Press International reporters, Lucinda Franks and Thomas Powers, researched and wrote the story of her life under the title "The Making of a Terrorist." The reporters chronicled her transformation from a wealthy, cheerful, and well-liked young lady into a truculent and uncompromising terrorist.

As a student at the University of Michigan, Diana Oughton became involved with the Weathermen faction of the Students for a Democratic Society, which was called "The Jesse James Gang." The gang declared themselves to be revolutionary gangsters and urged individual violent confrontations. They became known as "the action freaks" and the "crazies." Diana was one of a dozen Weatherwomen who plunged into the police lines in Chicago's Grant Park during "the days of rage."

According to the two reporters, one of Diana's male friends "who had started Diana thinking seriously about revolution in Guatemala, now found himself in the awkward position of trying to restrain her, to convince Diana that a premature attempt to bring on the revolution would be suicidal. Diana insisted the time had come to fight . . ."

Diana's boyfriend was a young man named Bill Ayers, described as "charming, manipulative, and a bit cruel." The pair shared an apartment in Ann Arbor. Their relationship, we are told, was—not surprisingly—turbulent, and a good case might be made for the notion that their stormy relationship was father to the violence that they both suicidally sought. Indeed, their revolutionary zeal began almost from the moment they met one another. The longer they lived together, the more bloodthirsty they became.

Bill Ayers was one of the Weathermen later indicted on bomb conspiracy charges. He was once asked what the Weathermen program was. "Kill all the rich people," he answered. "Bring the revolution home, kill your parents. That's where it's really at."

We are told that in Chicago, "Diana's relationship with Bill Ayers came under increasing strain . . . Ayers told Diana he would not allow himself to be tied to one woman, and she began spending her time with a number of other men." For a time she lived in a collective in Chicago. "The collectives attempted to destroy all their old attitudes about sexual relationships. The Women's Liberation caucus had proposed that Weathermen attempt to 'smash monogamy' on the grounds that it oppressed women and at the same time created love relationships which interfered with revolutionary commitment . . . As a result, long-established couples were sometimes ordered to separate, and sexual relations became mandatory between all members of a collective. Diana and Bill Ayers were one of the couples forced apart during this period . . . In some instances, homosexuality and lesbianism were involved."

Friends of Ayers, meantime, said he became interested in Bernardine Dohrn, one of the national officers of the Weathermen. They said Ayers "was increasingly fascinated by Bernardine's toughness, intelligence, and hard beauty . . ." This Bernardine Dohrn was the same woman who, at a war council of the Weathermen in Flint, Michigan, praised the alleged murderers of actress Sharon Tate and others. "Dig it!" she told the war council. "First they killed those pigs, then they ate dinner in the same room with them . . ."

In February, 1971, the University of Michigan's graduate assembly released the results of a survey of student opinion. The study reported that 45.2 percent of the students interviewed believed that violence was sometimes justified to achieve certain ends. The breakdown by sex was especially interesting. Only 3.9 percent of the males, but 5 percent of the females, felt that disruption of classes and research was *absolutely* justified in many circumstances. Only 36.9 percent of the males, but as many as 50.1 percent of the females, felt that violence was justified in some cases when other methods of calling attention to grievances have apparently failed. About 35.5 percent of the males, but only 28.8 percent of the females, said that violence was seldom justified.

Often the victims of female violence are other females, especially female teachers. On May 10, 1971, in Ann Arbor, a twenty-four-year-old Forsythe Junior High School teacher, Mrs. Mary Ann Otsuji, was severely beaten by a thirteen-year-old female student whom the teacher had tried to order out of her classroom. Five days later in the Bronx, Miss Georgette McNair, a twenty-four-year-old teacher in Public School 73, was hospitalized with second-degree burns after three female students—one fifteen and the other two thirteen—set her clothing on fire. The police said the students, who were charged with attempted murder, had tried unsuccessfully earlier in the week to push the teacher down a staircase at the school.

Nonetheless, the University of Michigan's current administration continues to cower before the strident demands of the campus liberationists. Shortly before the survey findings were released, the university invited Professor Germaine Bree, a University of Wisconsin French literature scholar, to give the first commencement address ever delivered by a woman at the university. The Women's Liberation Movement is "a meaningful and desirable social commitment," Professor Bree declared. "We women need to be obstinate," she said. The publicity release on Professor Bree's speech did not include the intriguing facts that she: (1) had served in the French army; (2) was an authority on André Gide, the French homosexual; and (3) was never married.

The triangular relationship between feminism, homosexuality, and violence was never made clearer than in the movie *Bonnie and Clyde*, which was, not surprisingly, a big box-office attraction. In that context, consider the observation of Faye Dunaway, who played Bonnie, when she was interviewed recently in Spain: "Something happens to me when I'm here. I never enjoy being a woman as much as I do when I'm in Europe . . . It's something to do with the way women are treated here, I suppose. European men are so much gentler and kinder than their counterparts in America. It's because American men feel so threatened by their women, I think. It's not the same at all in Europe. Even when you're whistled at in Europe, it's different from the way you're whistled at in America."

"Chivalry," says one Women's Liberationist, "is a cheap price to pay for power." And it appears that the courts are in agreement. In ordering the doors of the all-male saloon,

McSorely's in New York, open to women, District Court Judge Walter R. Mansfield commented, "Without suggesting that chivalry is dead, we no longer hold to Shakespeare's immortal phrase, 'Frailty, thy name is woman.'"

THE LOCKHORNS

"YOU HEAR A BURGLAR? WHY DON'T YOU GO DOWNSTAIRS AND SCARE HIM OFF?"

It is a fact that the less womanlike the American female has become, the more warlike the American male has become. Helen Dudar notes in *Newsweek* that, in the Women's Liberation Movement, "there is a fidgety expectation of eventual backlash, supported even now by an occasional burst of male violence."

American men are terrified of the American woman, with good reason. As an example of the fear that the modern woman inspires in the bravest of men, I cite the fact that many men wrote to the Society for the Emancipation of the American Male expressing their enthusiastic support, but at the same time added, as one male did, "Please do not follow this up in any way, as it may lead to difficulty for me that I would not be prepared to cope with." It was clear that many men who were happy at news of the formation of SEAM refused nonetheless to join because of their wives.

One male crusader for divorce reform was afraid for his life. We received the following letter from George F. Doppler, Central East Coast regional director of United States Divorce Reform, Inc.:

"The fact is, the divorce court system has our people in a living HELL. Today's courts do not administer justice. They are used for persecution! Most of the fathers who 'disappear' do so not at the onset of their marital problem, but *after* confrontation with the court system, often where he can't speak his side equally, or is even permitted to speak.

"A Passaic County couple was convicted on fornication charges. The male was sentenced to three months, the female six months, but the sentence was suspended for her! This is what we call equal justice in the U.S. What other charge could have been more equal between sexes?

"One of our members has asked for help and protection. He has asked that if he suddenly disappears, or is subject to any personal attack, we are to go into action. A local person will keep day-by-day and hour-by-hour watch over him, and will notify this address should anything happen. He also asks that we notify the Associated Press, NBC, and CBS.

"Good thing we have so many trained and battle-experienced veterans in divorce reform. This man needs help. If you did any form of duty that could be helpful at this time, let us know. Like intelligence work, demolition experts in the event of bomb threats, military police for protection guards . . .

"He says he is getting 'tap' interference on telephone conversations, so watch your talk on the phone. Three of his members have had their lives threatened, and one attempt to wreck his auto, plus some minor incidents . . ."

But there is still hope. Buried in the report of the National Commission on the Causes and Prevention of Violence was the following observation, which went largely unnoticed by the press:

"If discontented groups regard their social environment as completely overpowering and threatening, they are likely to withdraw defensively and to establish barriers that preserve their cultural identity by minimizing their relations with the larger society. Such defensive withdrawals have been attempted in the United States, for instance, by the Mormons, the Amish, and the Black Muslims."

The Violence Commision failed to point out—perhaps because it was not aware of the social structure of these groups—that the Mormons, the Amish, and the Black Muslims are all fiercely patriarchal, religious organizations which have deliberately fled the matriarchal madness surrounding them —a phenomenon of no small significance.

Famous People Speak Out in Support of Samra's Law

The truth of Samra's Law was the same yesterday as it is today, and it shall be so forever. There is some evidence that Cato was aware of it. In 195 B.C. Cato declared, "The moment they begin to be your equals, they shall be your superiors." An old Korean proverb says: A family with the voice of woman heard louder than man is doomed to failure.

More recently, some of America's great writers have spoken out in support of Samra's Law.

Says Russell Lynes: "Man, once known as 'the head of the family,' is now partner in the family firm, part-time mother and part-time maid. He is the chief cook and bottle washer, the chauffer, the gardener, and the houseboy; the maid, the laundress, and the charwoman . . . Today's husbands are the new servant class."

Declares Philip Wylie: "This calamity has befallen us in a

mere quarter-century. Before that the male aura dominated a society dreamed up by males, by males pioneered, made free and kept united by males—a culture still sustained by males in the main, but men whose sweating effort nowadays lops a decade off their lives that the damsels do not sacrifice . . .''

Says Edward Grossman: "In the street the male faces are mild. The fiercest physiognomies belong to homosexuals, and to women . . . Is it because I have some fear of women that I seem to suggest that the new egalitarianism in bed is going to smash society?"

THE LOCKHORNS

"I'M NOT INCOMPATIBLE! YOU ARE!"

Said John Steinbeck: "Once a man married a woman younger than himself because her term of life, due to work and childbearing, was shorter than his. But the pressures of present-day American life, particularly on men in the business world, make it almost the rule that the husband dies first. The result is a great oversupply of widows. It is the

American man's duty to live and act in the almost certain knowledge that his wife will survive him."

"Women," said Alexander King, "are sitting like district attorneys to see what the man can or cannot perform."

Says Morton Hunt: "The karate experts would like us to believe that physical differences between the sexes are merely a matter of different life-styles. But there has never been a culture of women that was as tall or strong as men. Either these women haven't read their biology or they discredit it because it doesn't fit their arguments."

Representative Emanuel Celler (D, N.Y.) agrees: "There is as much difference between a male and a female as there is between a horse chestnut and a chestnut horse," says Celler. "Vive la différence."

Cary Grant, whose recent divorce was a painful one, says he is going to give the following advice to his young daughter: "I'm going to tell her to find one man and make it her life's work to keep him happy. I'm going to tell her to forget being a modern woman with a career and all that nonsense. If there's one thing that I can instill in her mind, it will be that she must be dependent on her man for happiness—and she must stay at home and make it her castle."

Dr. Paul Popenoe, president of the American Institute of Family Relations, on Kate Millett's book *Sexual Politics*: "Evidently she thinks it is no longer desirable for the human race to perpetuate itself, because she wants to abolish the family, the only organization by which the race has ever perpetuated itself over any extended period of time. Cynics may say that the book is perhaps useful because it will eliminate from the stream of evolution those who accept its doctrines and will let mankind be perpetuated by more normal men and women."

Evangelist Billy Graham declared recently that "the Bible teaches that women have a role, that it is a noble role, a God-given role, and they will be happiest, most creative—and freest—when they assume and accept that role . . . Throughout history there has been very little deviation from the pattern. And when society has tried to merge the sexes into one, and has failed to recognize their basic and important differences, serious consequences have ensued. Wife, mother, homemaker, this is the appointed destiny of real womanhood. It can be embroidered on and supplemented, but the fabric underneath must be preserved. This is the Judeo-Christian ethic. After talking with hundreds of American women, I am convinced that the overwhelming majority want to remain feminine—and to be what they were meant to be."

Foreigners especially have viewed the American matriarchy with alarm. "Women wear the pants in America," observes Ida Monn, president of the League of Swiss Women Against Women's Suffrage. "Their slogan is 'Make War, Not Love—Take the Man's Job.' American women leave nothing sacred to their men. We don't want that kind of equality. We can't risk destroying man's role in the world. We must give him a task to perform . . . allow him to be chivalrous."

Declares Sir Harold Nicholson: "The American man belongs to the American woman. His wretched state fills me with rage at finding a person so deserving and honest subjected to a monstrous servitude; and pity that (owing partly to ignorance and partly to lack of character) he is unaware of his own degradation. He does not even recognize his tyrants. He finds them sweet and pretty little things; he is wholly unaware that he is being ground underfoot by one of the most heartless and ruthless tyrannies which civilization has ever witnessed . . .

"The American woman imagines that the men like it. She begins her career while she is still a child. She is a smarty to her parents, and to her brothers she is patronizing, sniffy, and occasionally downright mean . . . At college she will cease to be womanly and become male . . . Gradually she will merge into the mother and then the matron type. And when she dies, she will be regretted (though not for very long) by all those whom she has bound so cunningly with silken cords. Her husband, at that date, will be very rich, very ill indeed, but much relieved."

THE LOCKHORNS

"YES, I REALIZE YOU'VE GONE THROUGH A LOT IN OUR MARRIAGE ···· LIKE ALL MY MONEY!"

Says Malcolm Bradbury: "One of the deepest traumas experienced by every Englishman who comes to America is that of encountering for the first time, in quantity and in her own native habitat, the American woman . . . It should be remembered that American women are, from the European point of view, men. Years of emancipation have given American womenfolk personalties, opinions, leisure, money, careers, and all the other characteristics of male power. At the same time, male authority has been diminished, male spending power has been reduced, and all fathers have been symbolically slaughtered."

"The American woman is a man," according to Oriana Fallaci. "In Moslem countries, the women wear the veils. In America, the man wears the veil."

Actress Monica Vitti complains that "so many men are becoming like women that the only defense is for women to become like men."

C. Northcote Parkinson believes, "The trouble in American colleges is based on disrespect for authority. The general movement, I think, began with the female revolution. Women demanded the vote and equality and ceased to submit to the control of their husbands. In the process, they began to lose control of their own children. In my childhood, father's word was law, and mother's most deadly threat was: 'I shall have to inform your father.' Nowdays, mothers can't appeal to children in that way because they have denied the paternal authority themselves."

"Women rule the United States. American men have turned over everything to their wives. This is the greatest handover in history. Women and prosperity are at the root of most Americans' troubles." Or so says the British psychiatrist Joshua Bierer.

Sophia Loren says she has no use for Women's Liberation. "Being a sex symbol: What's wrong with it?" she asks. "A woman shouldn't forget her duties and responsibilities as a woman."

In Tokyo recently Malaysian Premier Tengku Abdul Rahman praised Japanese Prime Minister Eisaku Sato for beating his wife in the early days of their marriage. Rahman observed that wife beating gained Sato "unqualified popularity and support from many a browbeaten and less courageous husband. On the other hand, what the wives thought about it did not matter very much."

(When an American tries to beat his wife, however, it's another matter. Mrs. June M. Mavity of West Hartford, Connecticut, was awarded a divorce on grounds that her engineer husband claimed "divine right" to beat her.)

"It will be remarked," notes Gustave Le Bon, "that among the special characteristics of crowds there are several—such as impulsiveness, irritability, incapacity to reason, the absence of judgment and of the critical spirit, the exaggeration of the sentiments, and others besides—which are almost always observed in beings belonging to inferior forms of evolution—in women, savages, and children, for instance."

It is an encouraging sign that many women, too, see the truth of Samra's Law.

"I'm not a Women's Liberationist," says Sally Kellerman. "I want a man to run my house. When a burglar comes, I want *him* to go downstairs."

"Competition doesn't become women as a rule," according to Mrs. Billy Graham. "I was going to say, 'why compete when you can be superior.' "

"I prefer to have the strong arms of a man around me," declares Shirley Temple Black.

"They're [the girls in Women's Liberation] going to end up being unhappy women," predicts Nancy Reagan. "Part and parcel of being a woman is to be a mother and a homemaker . . . It's part of being a man to be a breadwinner and provider for your family. If you mix the two together, and make them one, you have unhappy people. They cheat themselves out of one of the great experiences of being a woman, I think."

Declares Mary Hemingway: "You see, here wives are so hardly ever gentle with their husbands, so rarely admiring. All their stupid talks on equality! Equality, what does it mean? What's the use for it? I've said it before and I'll repeat: Women are second-class citizens, and not only biologically. A female's first duty is to bear children and rear them . . . Equality! I didn't want to be Ernest's equal. I wanted him to be the master."

"I've always depended on men," says Ann-Margret. "I don't want to compete with them . . . If a woman does become a success . . . I just hope for her sake she has a strong man to come home to who will dominate her and make her feel she's still a woman."

Says Mrs. Spiro T. Agnew: "I just want to be a good wife. I don't think I need to be liberated."

"I really don't think women should vote," says Gussie Moran. "The man in the family should vote. I hope we never see a woman President . . . she'd be too emotional!"

"We want to pamper our husbands," insists Mrs. Marylou Cowham, president of the Pussycat Club of Louth, England. "They are the breadwinners and should come home to a nice, loving, all-female wife."

Mrs. Joan Rosanove, one of Australia's leading divorce lawyers, blames women for nineteen of every twenty marriage breakdowns. "Admittedly," she says, "there's always the man who is no good, but he's a rarity compared with the woman. Women don't work on the job of making the man happy."

"No, I'm not in favor of Women's Liberation," says Lucille Ball. "I don't have anything I want to be liberated from."

Kim Darby: "I don't think women as a group will ever be equal with men, and in some ways I don't think that's bad. I still like the feeling of being a lady and having doors opened for me."

"I didn't start out opposing the Women's Liberation Movement," remarks Mrs. Helen Andelin, a Santa Barbara mother of eight who recently promoted a national "Celebration of Womanhood" day. "But when I realized that Women's Lib was destroying our femininity that men love so much, I started speaking out against the Movement."

Finally, both black men and white men, though they agree on little else, have given testimonials as to the truth of Samra's Law:

"Women ain't supposed to be equal," declares Cassius Clay (now Muhammad Ali).

"The position of women in our movement (SNCC) should be prone," declares Stokeley Carmichael.

Says Johnny Cash: "To make a good man and to keep a good man, you got to have a good woman."

THE LOCKHORNS

"WELL, YOU SHOULD HAVE REALIZED I WAS STUPID WHEN I ASKED YOU TO MARRY ME!"

The Fall
of Matriarchies

"Men who live under the sway of their womenkind do not sustain great empires in the face of the bitter hostility of the most influential organized bodies in the realm." So remarked historian H. G. Wells about the ephemeral reign of the Egyptian Pharaoh Akhenaten.

The male reaction to the feminization of a society has not infrequently been swift and violent, if not downright psychotic. Archeologists recently uncovered and photographed the buried remains of the great Aten Temple, built by Akhenaten, a substantial part of it in honor of his wife, Queen Nefertiti. They were surprised to discover that decorations on the pillars in the courtyard of the temple consisted exclusively of likenesses of Queen Nefertiti and her princesses. They said the decorations "composed an extravagant and splendid exaltation of femininity. The pillars of this particular courtyard bore not a single figure of Akhenaten, nor even any inscriptional mention of him. In fact, nothing masculine—not a courtier, a fan bearer, or even a male animal—appears on the pillar blocks." Scenes of Nefertiti facing herself across an offering table, endlessly repeated, embellish all the pillars. "Such a tribute," noted the archeologists, "was never accorded any other Egyptian queen, before or after Nefertiti."

The archeologists found evidence that Nefertiti held divine status even at an early age. She was regarded as a goddess and prayers were addressed to her. But the pharaoh and his queen were not, apparently, happily married. Wells notes that Akhenaten was by his contemporaries known as the "gloomy fanatic," and "matrimonial bliss is rare in the cases of gloomy fanatics."

During Nefertiti's reign Egypt degenerated into chaos. The Aten regime collapsed. Horemheb marched on the temple and proclaimed himself pharaoh. What did the new pharaoh do? He supervised the desecration of the stones in Nefertiti's courtyard. Centuries later the archeologists were astonished to discover that all of the pillars had been turned upside down. The carved female figures had been mutilated. Their facial features, bodies, limbs, and fingers were hacked away. Curiously, the archeologists rarely found defacements on other pillar blocks on which male figures had been carved. Horemheb's legions, the archeologists speculated, possibly "intended to crush Nefertiti symbolically and to inflict on this beautiful creature the indignity of being turned upside down. She was expected to be lost forever from men's sight."

Another goddess, Aphrodite, the Greek goddess of love, apparently suffered a smiliar fate. The shattered marble head of the Aphrodite of Cnidus, the nude statue carved by Praxiteles in the fourth century B.C., was discovered recently by an archeologist in the basement of the British Museum. The head was badly defaced—minus its nose, mouth, and chin and a rear section of the skull and hairdo, as though somebody had hacked away at it continuously.

Apparently the same emotions that drove Egyptian men to deface Nefertiti's statue centuries before Christ, resurfaced centuries after Christ among Greek men and resulted in the mutilation of Aphrodite. So it has been throughout history as goddesses come and go, bringing war and violence in their wake.

Greek civilization, too, waxed and waned as it went from patriarchy to matriarchy and back again. The most warlike of the Greek city-states was Sparta where, Will Durant tells us, "the position of women was better than in any other Greek community." Plutarch observed that Spartan women "were bold and masculine, overbearing to their husbands . . . and speaking openly even on the most important subjects." Adds Durant: "In the course of time—so great was their influence over men—nearly half the real wealth of Sparta was in their hands."

Sparta was continually at war with its neighbors, and in 413 B.C. devastated Athens' manhood. Over the din of the misery and chaos are heard the laments of the Greek poets and philosophers, decrying the growing influence of women and the evil wrought by them. In Athens, the poet Hesiod declares that from Pandora "is the race of tender women; from her is a pernicious race; and tribes of women, a great hurt, dwell with men, helpmates not of consuming poverty but of surfeit . . . so to mortal man Zeus gave women as an evil." Writes Hesiod:

> No better lot has Providence assigned
> Than a fair woman with a virtuous mind;

Nor can a worse befall than when thy fate
Allots a worthless, feast-continuing mate,
She with no touch of mere material flame
Shall burn to tinder thy care-wasted frame;
Shall send a fire thy vigorous bones within
And age unripe in bloom of years begin.

Semonides of Amorgos compared women to foxes, asses, pigs, and the changeful sea, and declared that no husband ever went through a day without some criticism or nagging from his wife. Hipponax of Ephesus declared that a woman brings two days of happiness to her husband—"one when he marries her, the other when he buries her." Euripides insisted that woman is handicapped by lack of intellect. Aristophanes poked fun at the feminists of his day.

Durant tells us that the classic Greeks considered romantic love a form of "possession" or "madness" and that the Greek "prates endlessly" about the tribulations of marriage.

As Greece declined into anarchy and war, the numbers of bachelors and homosexuals increased by leaps and bounds. Once again, there is an attempt to regain control, to reestablish patriarchal authority, and the male philosophers come to Greece's rescue. Aristotle declares: "Woman is to man as the slave to the master, the barbarians to the Greek. The male is by nature superior, and the female inferior; the one rules and the other is ruled." Again: "The courage of a man is shown in commanding; the courage of a woman in obeying . . . As the poet says, 'Silence is a woman's glory.' " Aristotle advises a man to defer marriage until he is at least thirty-seven, and then to marry a girl of twenty.

Laws are passed to push woman back into the home, to get her out of the marketplace. Divorce laws are reformed so that it is more difficult for a woman to get a divorce, and the father is always awarded custody of the children. "So," says Durant, "the male is exalted by the theory popular in classic Greece that the generative power belongs to man, the woman being merely the carrier and nurse of the child."

Durant is astonished at how well Greece manages without women being involved in its business and public life. "As surprising as anything else in this civilization [Athens] is the fact that it is brilliant without the aid of women. With their help the Heroic Age achieved splendor, the age of the dictators a lyric radiance; then almost overnight, married women vanish from the history of the Greeks, as if to confute the supposed correlation between the level of civilization and the status of woman. In Herodotus woman is everywhere; in Thucydides she is nowhere to be seen. From Semonides of Amorgos to Lucian, Greek literature is offensively repetitious about the faults of women; and towards the close of it even the kindly Plutarch repeats Thucydides: 'The name of a decent woman, like her person, should be shut up in the house.' "

But what's so surprising? Islam attained the height of its glory, the apex of its civilization, without the aid of women. So did Judaism. So, too, did Buddhism, Hinduism, and Christianity.

It was not long, however, before things came full circle again in Greece, and the feminists reestablished themselves. Anarchy reigned once more, and the Greeks responded by giving themselves Alexander. The brilliant young homosexual promptly took them to war, conquering half the world before succumbing to a fever at an early age. Thereafter, the decline of Greece was rapid, and the land was easily conquered by the Romans.

In Judea a couple centuries later, similar forces were at work. The decline of Judea was accelerated under the reign of the ruthless and bloodthirsty King Herod, who was having problems with his various wives. Durant tells us Herod managed to foil "all his enemies except his wives and his children." His second wife, Marianne, "treated her husband imperiously because she saw he was so fond of her as to be her slave." Herod was convinced that she was trying to poison him and had her executed. Later, he became quite feverish and descended into madness.

Rome, meantime, was going the way of Greece. "The extinction of faith in the familistic system [in America]," says Harvard Professor Emeritus Carle Zimmerman, "is identical with the movements in Greece during the century following the Peloponnesian wars, and in Rome from about A.D. 150. In each case, the change in the faith and belief in family systems was associated with rapid adoption of negative reproduction rates and with enormous crises in the very civilizations themselves."

In the last days of the Roman Empire, Rome was, in effect, ruled by women. The degenerate Roman Emperor Elagabulus was emperor in name only. In fact, his mother, the Syrian Julia Soaemias, was the ruler. This was a period of great turmoil. The Roman Guard slew both Elagabulus and his mother, and installed his cousin Alexander as emperor, only to discover that Alexander's mother was ruling behind the scenes. So the Guard rebelled and slew Alexander and his mother. The Goths, the barbarians, and the Germans poured in from the north, pillaging and looting.

Especially brutal and especially fierce were the Germans. The Roman historian Tacitus observed that war was the meat and drink of the Germans, and he described the enthusiasm with which the German women urged their men on to battle and fought by their side.

Centuries later a student of history, Samuel Johnson, who saw things clearly, was to declare to a friend, "Sir, nature has given woman so much power that the law cannot afford to give her more."

It is clear that the rise and fall of civilizations is intimately related to the woman question. History tells us that all civilizations have declined into anarchy when women have abandoned the home for the marketplace. The response of society is invariably either the rise of a military dictatorship or a religious revival. Let us pray that the reaction to the feminists of this century will be led not by the militarists and the psychotics, but by men of faith and good will.

The Case for Witchcraft

The preachers warned us about all this a century ago. The early nineteenth-century clergy denounced the early feminists from their pulpits as witches and instruments of the devil. But not many people listened. For many Americans the belief in witches was passé because, after all, this was the Age of Enlightenment. Nobody talked about witches again until the late nineteen-sixties when the term was revived, this time not by preachers, but by a growing army of divorced men, male deserters, homosexuals, psychotics, bachelors, misogynists, and, oddly enough, latter-day feminists. And, lo and behold, all at once people started believing in witches again.

Not long after SEAM's formation, we received a letter from a Catholic priest who had abandoned his vows of celibacy and gotten married. The priest reported gloomily that he is now separated after less than a year of what turned out to be a turbulent marriage. He advised his fellow priests who are eager to leave the safety of the priesthood for marriage to stay put and stay celibate. "They just don't know what they're getting into," wrote the priest, and he ended by predicting that, at the present pace of the feminist movement, the twentieth century will see a revival of the age-old belief in witchcraft.

THE LOCKHORNS

"ARENT YOU WEARING A COSTUME TO THE PARTY?"

"For out of the womb of the modern-day feminist," the priest wrote in a theological seizure, "issue all manner of evils: madmen, suicidal men, homosexuals, divorced men, deserters, confirmed bachelors, criminals, misogynists, unemployed men, dead men . . ."

The priest's case, written in a moment of anger, may perhaps be somewhat overstated. But it is curious that all of a sudden the Witches' International Terrorist Conspiracy from Hell (WITCH) has made its appearance in several cities, an extension of the Women's Liberation Movement. Books are appearing like *Power Through Witchcraft* (Louise Heubner) and *Mastering Witchcraft, A Practical Guide for Witches, Warlocks, & Covens* (Paul Huson), and are finding a ready market.

Susan Brownmiller, writing in *The New York Times Magazine*, explains how the WITCH organization got started: "Several women felt the need for a new group. They had become intrigued with the role of the witch in world history as representing society's persecution of women who dared to be different. From Joan of Arc, who dared to wear men's clothes and lead a men's army, to the women of Salem, who dared to defy accepted political, religious mores, the 'witch' was punished for deviations. Out of this thinking grew WITCH, a handy acronym that the organizers announced, half tongue-in-cheek, stood for Women's International Terrorist Conspiracy from Hell."

But perhaps even more significant is the popular revival of the term itself. "My father died when I was twelve," recalled the late Judy Garland, "and my mother was no good for anything except to create chaos and fear. She was the worst —the real-life Wicked Witch of the West."

At the trial of cult leader Charles Manson and three of the girl friends in his "family," accused of murdering actress Sharon Tate, Linda Kasabian testified that when Manson ordered her to the Tate home, he told them to " 'leave a sign.' He said, 'You girls know what I mean—something witchy.' " Miss Kasabian said Manson referred to girls in his mostly female clan as "witches."

After Washington newswomen gave England's Princess Anne such a difficult time during her recent visit, the British press roundly denounced the American ladies as witches. Said

The People: "The ladies of the press—some say they turn up for work on broomsticks—made nineteen-year-old Anne's sight-seeing tour a sheer misery." *The People* denounced the newshens as "witches," "harpies," and "ill-mannered rag-bags." The *Sunday Mirror* chimed in with "everywhere that Anne went, the 'witches' went, too—pushing and shoving the Princess and trying to ask questions."

In England, according to *Presbyterian Life*, what started out as a laughing matter is no longer funny. Anglican rectors, the magazine reports, are getting increasingly concerned about "more and more rumors and tales of strange clandestine meetings, weird rites, and prayers to Lucifer, the prince of darkness. In some cases, witchcraft in England is getting about as funny as it was once in Salem, Massachusetts. What has been happening beyond a shadow of a doubt is that graves are being disturbed. In some cases bodies are being removed and the bones scattered; chapels are being broken into and black magic symbols left behind."

Marcello Truzzi, assistant professor of sociology at the University of Michigan, an instructor in witchcraft and author of *Caldron Cookery*, informed us that there are now about two hundred witches' covens in the United States. "A lot of college girls get into witchcraft," says Truzzi. "The witch is typically a young girl of high school or college age who has self-designated herself a witch to her peers for a variety of reasons, probably because it is attractive to her friends and fear-provoking in her enemies." About 225 people, 60 percent of them women, signed up for his course in witchcraft, black magic, and modern occultism. Truzzi, incidentally, is the chap who discovered a new psychiatric ailment which he calls polyanoia, or "the outrageous belief that one is not being persecuted."

The New York Times devoted considerable space to a report on the growth of witches' cults and the increasing popularity of courses in sorcery and witchcraft on college campuses. Not long ago a Catholic university discovered a coven of warlocks (male witches) on its campus. Commented the dean: "We've really become progressive around here. A couple of hundred years ago, we would have burned them at the stake. Twenty-five years ago, I would have expelled them. Now we simply sent them all to psychiatrists."

Whether the church can cope with the witches in its own ranks remains to be seen. The high-pitched voices of rebellion are being heard throughout the church:

"Some day soon," warns Dr. Elizabeth Farians, professor of theology at Loyola University of Chicago, "some pastor is going to tell a woman she can't read the epistle and she's going to pop him one. We're not encouraging it, but it's going to happen. The women are enraged."

Declared the National Coalition of American Nuns: "We protest any domination of our institution by priests, no matter what their hierarchical status. We defend ourselves against those who would interfere with the internal administration and/or renewal that we alone must and can evolve in our religious community."

Said Mrs. Betty Schiess, an Episcopal theology student, "I do take the church seriously. I don't for one minute belittle its teachings. It's just that where women are concerned, they don't apply."

Dr. Nelle Morton, a Presbyterian theologian, declared that it was blasphemy to speak of divine love as *he*, and advised churchmen to try on such labels as "househusband" or "callboy."

Betty Friedan told a New York audience: "The great

debate of the sixties was 'Is God dead?' I think the great debate of the seventies will be 'Is God he?' "

The tone of the feminist rebellion within the church is vaguely reminiscent of the eighteenth and nineteenth centuries, which witnessed the birth of a number of female-led religions. Most notably, Christian Science, the Seventh-Day Adventists, and the Shakers. All three of the female founders —Mary Baker Eddy, Ellen G. White, and Ann Lee—had been pampered and raised indulgently by their parents. All three had turbulent marriages. (Mary Baker Eddy had three of them.) All three suffered from a variety of mental and physical ailments throughout their lives. All three were prone to seizures of hysteria. ("I have been a great sufferer from disease, having had five shocks of paralysis," said Ellen White.) All three were obsessed with the great questions of sickness and health, and formulated their own health systems. ("When the message of health reform first came to me" said Ellen White, "I was weak and feeble, subject to frequent fainting spells . . . I have had a great light from the Lord upon the subject of health reform.") All three were militant feminists. Each had a vision that she was the second Christ. (Ann Lee advised her Shaker followers to give up marriage.) Finally, all three were denounced as witches by the clergy and men of their times.

Ann Lee's life was a psychiatric case history of psychedelic proportions. Her four children died in infancy. She was frequently found dancing and shouting in the streets and was imprisoned for breaking the Sabbath and for blasphemy. She continually had trances and visions. She gathered around her a group of followers who were sometimes called the Shaking Quakers but later merely the "Shakers," because they writhed and trembled, jumped and danced in order to free the soul from the power of sin and worldly life.

Ann Lee called herself "Ann, the Word," and her followers believed she was the second coming of Christ. Ann insisted that God is a bisexual, and the bisexuality of the Creator required that there be an equal number of elders and elderesses, deacons and deaconesses in the church. The Shakers were fanatic advocates of sex equality. They also refused to recognize marriage as a Christian institution and practiced celibacy.

Ann Lee brought her followers from England to America in 1774. Her husband soon deserted her, and she died at the youthful age of forty-eight, a troubled woman. The Shakers founded a number of colonies in America, but their numbers declined rapidly and many of them disappeared, as most feminist religious organizations do—sooner or later. Ann Lee was regarded as something of a witch by the clergy and commonfolk of her time, and this view was shared by her husband. Our initial response in this century is to laugh at such unscientific notions. But then our ideas on the subject of witchcraft have been largely shaped by modern writers who scoff at this ancient belief and who, in their writings, can always be found on the side of the witches, acting as their apologists, explaining them away as harmless schizophrenics. The talented Arthur Miller, for instance, has taken the side of the witches in writing sympathetically about the Salem witch trials. But that was some time ago, and we wonder whether the troubles that Marilyn Monroe and his three marriages gave him have changed his view. Indeed, another authority on the Salem witch trials has just come out with a book providing evidence that there *were* witches in Salem, that they *were* deadly, and that they deserved what they got.

In any case, the belief in witchcraft is too entrenched among all civilizations to dissipate so easily. For centuries, in all civilizations, people—both dull and brilliant—have believed that women were capable of raising the devil by means of spells and forcing him to do their will. In every civilization magical powers have been attributed to women. The Thessalian women of ancient Greece were famous for their poisons. In medieval Europe women were believed to be able to cast the "evil eye." In many parts of the world female demons were regarded as being especially malignant. And these demons were generally identified with female deities.

Greek mythology is especially rich in references to women —both goddesses and witches—as troublemakers. Indeed, both the Greek account of the creation and Genesis agree on one point: when God (Zeus) first created the world, only men lived upon the earth, and nary a woman was in sight. The Greeks called it the glorious Golden Age; the Hebrews called it the Garden of Eden. And in both cases, the fall of man resulted after the creation of woman and her succumbing to temptations that spawned all manner of evils down through the centuries. Hence the legend of Pandora's box.

The gods gave Pandora, a fair maiden, a box in which many harmful things had been placed, and sent her to earth. She was forbidden to open it, just as it was forbidden Eve to eat the apple, but curiosity got the best of Pandora, and one day she opened the box. Plagues, sorrow, and all kinds of misfortune, disasters, and evil for mankind flew out.

Like Hitler, the ancient Greeks also recognized the relationship between war and love. In their mythology, Ares (Mars), the god of war, always took sides with Aphrodite, the goddess of love, and he is sometimes seen as the lover of Aphrodite. Mars is always followed by a retinue which includes his sister Eris, or Discord. And the Greeks also had a goddess of war, Enyo, who walks alongside Mars accompanied by Terror, Trembling, and Panic. Mars' daughters are the Amazons, the bloodthirsty warriors. Rather than do battle with them, Jason and the Argonauts hurried past the Amazons in their quest for the golden fleece.

After Hecules' wife, Princess Megara, bore him three sons, the strongest man in the world went mad. He killed both his wife and his children and, strangely, his sanity immediately returned. In order to do penance, Hercules then set out on the dangerous adventures of the Twelve Labors.

The stories of Oedipus and of Helen of Troy also clearly show that the Greeks were quite understanding of the terrible passions unleashed by women. The Sirens, who lived on an island, were said to possess enchanting voices, and their singing lured sailors to their deaths. No one who saw them ever returned. Piles of skeletons surrounded them on the shore where they sang. When his ship was passing the island of the Sirens, Odysseus instructed his men to seal their ears with wax, lest they hear them and be lured to their deaths.

In many civilizations it was popularly supposed that witches could cause impotence in men by magical means ("ligature"). In medieval times theologians, pressed by suits for divorce or marriage nullification, believed that witchcraft was a cause of impotence. Centuries later, Freud was to discover the awesome psychosexual damage inflicted by male-mothers and male-wives on their sons and husbands. Impotence in men, Freud claimed, was indeed caused by women, and the formidable figure of the "castrating woman" was invoked by psychiatrists and writers throughout the land, but no one associated the Freudian notion with the ancient belief in *impotentia ex maleficio*.

Interestingly, Islam also recognized the impotence problem, and in an illuminating passage the Koran warns that those who do not accept the true faith will not have children.

Another tenacious belief in medieval times was the belief in the female monster who kills children. This belief was widespread during the time of the Inquisition. Farfetched? Not according to the increasingly commonplace news reports of modern mothers going berserk and killing their children. Not long ago, a mentally disturbed Brooklyn mother drowned her four children in the bathtub. And what about the epidemic of emotionally disturbed children that now afflicts this country? The vast majority of them come from broken homes, many of them have been abandoned by their mothers, and all of them are suffering through the living death of mental illness.

The sanity of the medieval witches, like the sanity of the modern ones, was doubtful. They saw visions, they had trances, they had attacks of hysteria. Signs of the witch included the inability to cry or to blush or to feel physical pain—common schizophrenic symptoms. Authorities believe that the historical evidence for witchcraft is vast and varied. And historians suggest that the belief in witchcraft, as well as the number of witches at any given time, seemed to ebb and flow throughout history. At certain times great epidemics of witchcraft seemed to attack nations, and these times appear to have been when the institutions of the society had become largely feminized. Inevitably there was a sharp reaction to it.

Mosaic law declared witchcraft to be a crime and insisted that a witch should not be suffered to live (Exod. 22:18). Witchcraft was widespread at the time of Christ, and we find St. Paul warning the early Christians about it. Later, Augustine declared that witchcraft depends on a pact with the devil.

Witchcraft became so widespread and commonplace in medieval times that it clearly posed a threat to society and to the church. Society's response was the Inquisition, and anywhere from a hundred thousand to several million witches and supposed witches were tried and brutally persecuted in ways that were less than civilized. Many were burned at the stake. But the viciousness of the reaction suggests that these women had a lot of people terrified and in fact were causing a great deal of trouble.

THE LOCKHORNS

"GUESS WHAT, LEROY! MOTHER IS FLYING IN TONIGHT!"

Ann Lee had her modern counterpart in Aimee Semple McPherson. Sister Aimee, quite possibly, was a reincarnation of Ann Lee. Their lives had many parallels. Her father was a figure dimly seen, according to biographer Lately Thomas, and her mother, Minnie Kennedy, was "the archtypal theatrical mother, watchful, tight-fisted, ruthless."

Sister Aimee's first husband died young and her second

husband deserted her. She and her mother bought a tent and hit the camp-meeting trail. They prospered in the revival business, using all of the gimmicks of the professional theater—footlights, scenery, music, action. The evangelist once observed: "The people can't get anything at the theater that we haven't got." Thomas notes that followers of Sister Aimee found her to be in her private life a woman "deceitful and greedy for money and worldly pleasure."

Sister Aimee tried marriage a third time, but this one, too, failed, and she declared: "Jamais encore!" She died in September, 1944, of an overdose of barbiturates.

Today, the witches are still obsessed with the questions of health and disease, but the modern variety is more attracted to psychiatry than to religion. They are well versed in the language of psychiatry, and their visions are of themselves as Freud, not Christ.

In *McCall's* magazine, a former Catholic priest described his marriage two years ago to an Episcopalian divorcée. "It's been rough," said the ex-priest, William H. DuBay. "We're still not sure our marriage will survive." DuBay admitted that the many ex-priests who have married have special problems.

DuBay's marriage to the former Mary Ellen Rochester, thirty-one, has been troubled from the start. He said his marriage was a battleground. Sometimes, he said, "I would go into a rage, once even ordering her to her room . . . We fought in front of the children, friends, strangers in the house, behind the barn, in the car, and in the middle of town . . ."

Finally, DuBay said, his wife gave him an ultimatum which should not surprise most married men who read "Dear Abby"—either divorce or see a psychiatrist. Like thousands of other American men, DuBay meekly chose to see a psychiatrist. He is now under therapy.

(An Oriental or a Greek man would have sent the wife to a psychiatrist, or better yet, simply ordered her out of the house and divorced her. And their countrymen and their courts would have backed them up, but that sort of thing happens only in backward and underdeveloped countries.)

Whether the revival of the belief in witchcraft will include witch-burning is anyone's guess. But what is clear is the increasingly popular recognition of a fact that all of the great religions have agreed upon, though they agreed upon little else, and that is that a woman can indeed, as the Koran unequivocally states, take a man either to heaven or to hell. Her powers for good or for evil are awesome. Everyone—from Vatsyayana, Isaiah, St. Paul, and Mohammed, to Norman Mailer, Cassius Clay, Tennessee Williams, and Edward Albee —has agreed on that point (though their solutions to the problem have been decidedly different).

Not long ago, a Woman's Liberationist suggested that the rules of poker playing be changed so that four queens beat four kings. So now you know why the Queen of Spades has been regarded for centuries as the deadliest card in the deck. Lest we forget, it was not a man's face that launched a thousand ships, nor a man's tongue that demanded the head of John the Baptist.

Samra's Principle:
How To Change Your Wife
Through Prayer

In America today we are rapidly reaching the nadir of a once-great civilization, having degenerated into a matri-archal-juvenile society run by women and children. Aristotle said much the same thing in the fourth century B.C. as he watched Greece descending into chaos. "Children," he observed, "are the rulers of their parents, and women find joy in men's clothing." Plutarch reported that men had taken to wearing bizarre costumes. Hashish and sex were "in." These were the conditions that produced Alexander the Great, the warrior, who is said on good authority to have been a mama's boy. Another great patriarchal civilization, Rome, was undergoing a similar decline about the time of Christ, and its institutions had been largely feminized. Indeed, the likelihood is that the feminists of ancient Greece and imperial Rome had more to do with the decline and fall of these two great civilizations than did the invading barbarians from the north.

THE LOCKHORNS

"IS THIS TO BE FOR A LOVED ONE, SIR······ OR YOUR WIFE?"

The signs are many that the last days are upon us in America. The FBI and criminologists report that female criminals and felons are on the increase. A Gallup survey found that one out of every four college women "participated in a demonstration of some kind." Harvard psychiatrist A. M. Nicholi reported to the American Psychiatric Association that students who had spent their teens in boarding schools and never knew their fathers were heavily overrepresented among Harvard demonstrators who had engaged in violent confrontations with the police. In another study of fifteen hundred Harvard dropouts, Dr. Nicholi found that twice as many had been separated from their fathers as was the case for the average student population. "Many youths come from homes in which the family unit has virtually disintegrated," Dr. Nicholi observed.

Organizations of many kinds proliferate in America, but while Americans, working with strangers, make great successes of their organizations, our families are all too often colossal disasters. Robert Townsend, former president of Avis and author of *Up the Organization*, concedes that he was "a disaster as a father. My eldest daughter is in the middle of a divorce from a Hollywood stunt man, the next is between lovers, another is going to work for Nader this summer, there's a nineteen-year-old son who's dropped out from everything for awhile and is very unhappy, and the youngest son is concerned about leaving school because they're cracking down on blowing pot. I ignored the hell out of my kids when they were younger. I take full responsibility for everything they do . . . I have told all the kids, every one of them, that if I had to do it all over again, I wouldn't have any because I am terrified of them."

Samra's Principle

All of the foregoing is in prelude to Samra's Corollary to Samra's Law, which I shall call Samra's Principle, and that is that:

Each of the great religions was born and grew out of circumstances where men had lost control over their women and children, and that one of the central aims of every religion was to elevate the male, subdue the woman, and rope in the kids. All of the great religions recognized women as troublemakers, and all of them sought, with varying degrees of success, to bring women to heel, to harmonize relations within the family, and to preserve the family.

Or, restated:

Men organize religions; women are the cause of them.

Hinduism and Women

Centuries before Christ, Hinduism was telling the people of India that women were troublemakers and held the power of life and death over men. Consider the following ancient Hindu proverbs, and then compare them with some of the Hebrew proverbs, the declarations of St. Paul, and the wisdom of the Koran:

A wife is not merely mate; she is entire fate.

A bad wife; an undependable friend; an insolent servant; a haunted house: these things mean death. (Note that a bad wife is first on the list.)

A treacherous wife would kill you and then share your pyre.

Woman is a pot of oil; man is a burning coal. Wise men do not put oil and fire together.

Trust not rivers; or animals with claws and horns; or men with weapons; or women with good looks.

From a debt to one's father, from a single daughter, and from traveling a mile alone may God preserve you.

A woman's glance is like a wicked person. It attaches itself to those who cannot control their senses, it diverts the mind's concentration, it moves crookedly like a poisonous snake, and carries itself proud and lofty.

The old woman makes a chaste wife.

But Hinduism also exalted good women and good wives. Hinduism's instructions to the faithful were to seek virtuous, modest, and obedient wives, and then to treat them well. Hindu women, in turn, were instructed to be good wives. Consider these proverbs, and again compare them to the Judaic, Christian, and Islamic traditions:

She is a worthy wife who cares for the welfare of her husband. Such a wife comes to men by good fortune alone.

In work a slave; in business a diplomat; in form a goddess; in intercourse a courtesan; in virtue firm as earth; in giving food like a mother: is she not a worthy wife?

She is a wife who is efficient in her house; she is a wife who is fruitful in her children; she is a wife who is cheering to her family; she is a wife who is obedient to her husband.

Modesty is the embellishment of women.

Misfortune is the touchstone by which a man discovers the character of his wife.

Judge a woman not by her charms but by her qualities.

THE LOCKHORNS

"I THINK OF ALL THE MEN YOU COULD HAVE MARRIED, TOO!"

Just as the happiest family was that family which was ruled by the father, the best government was that government which was ruled by men, according to the Hindu wise men:

A family survives by having one head, not many heads.

Those without a leader perish; those with a childish leader perish; those with a female leader perish; those with a multitude of leaders perish. (Compare this with the words of Isaiah, Paul, and Mohammed, which we shall shortly be examining.)

The Bhagavad-Gita, like the Old Testament, the New Testament, and the Koran, is a masculinist tract. And it was on this basis that Manu, the Indian lawgiver, laid down this law for Hindu women to follow: Whether a drunkard, a leper, a sadist, or a wife beater, a husband is to be worshipped as a God.

Centuries later, the Hindu patriarchal tradition found another expression in the writings of Vatsyayana. The *Kama Sutra* has enjoyed a popular revival recently in America among persons whom Vatsyayana himself would have scorned. For it is not generally known that the *Kama Sutra*, an analysis of the art of physical love, was addressed to married couples primarily and was written by a Hindu *theology student*.

Indeed, at the end of his work, Vatsyayana himself declares, "the *Kama Sutra* was composed, according to the precepts of the Holy Writ, for the benefit of the world by Vatsyayana, while leading the life of a religious student and wholly engaged in the contemplation of the Deity." Vatsyayana, by writing in detail about the arts of physical love, hoped, according to his expressed intention, to harmonize husband-wife relations, to improve their sexual performances, and thereby to preserve the institution of marriage, which he regarded as holy and sacred. But all of these things, he believed, depended on the supremacy of the male:

"A virtuous woman, who has affection for her husband,

should act in conformity with his wishes as if he were a divine being," he declared. "She should surpass all the women of her own rank in her manner of serving her husband."

"When a wife hears the sounds of her husband's footsteps coming home, she should at once get up and be ready to do whatever he may command her."

"Moreover, she should not be a scold, for, says Gonardiya, there is no cause of dislike on the part of a husband so great as this characteristic in a wife."

"She should not be vain, or too much taken up with her enjoyments."

"The wife, whether she be a woman of noble family, or a virgin widow remarried, or a concubine, should lead a chaste life, devoted to her husband, and doing everything for his welfare. Women acting thus acquire Dharma, Artha, and Karma, obtain a high position, and generally keep their husbands devoted to them."

Buddhism and Women

Buddhism was an offshoot of Hinduism, and though it parted company with its parent religion on several theological issues, it retained Hinduism's patriarchal traditions. Buddhism was from the beginning a masculinist movement. Indeed, Gotama the Buddha appeared at a time when the institutions of Hinduism had been feminized and had declined in popular appeal. The Brahmins had fallen into disrepute, and all India was torn by discord, rebellion, and war.

Doubtless, Buddha was also influenced by the teachings of

the great Chinese philosopher Confucius. Confucius was quite adamant in insisting that "the woman's duty is to prostrate herself submissively before her husband in such a way as to have no will of her own, but to demonstrate a perfect form of obedience." The Chinese clearly also had painful experiences with their women over the centuries, and inevitably these experiences gave birth to the concept of Yang and Yin. In Chinese lore, Yang represents the male or positive forces in life, and Yin represents the female or negative elements. Indeed, the early Chinese physicians built an elaborate form of medical treatment around this concept, called acupuncture, whereby needles were inserted into various parts of the body with the aim of curing a disease by influencing the pattern of the Yin and Yang forces.

Before he became the Buddha, Gotama was married and living a life of comparative ease. However, nowhere is it said that he was happily married, and the probability is that he was unable to tolerate his wife. Why else would a man leave his family, as Gotama did? It was while Gotama was married that he went into the streets and observed all of the pain and suffering to which man is heir. And it was after he had left his wife that he attained Nirvana, alone under the Bo Tree. Thereafter he preached the Noble Eightfold Path which was to end in the passing away of all pain and suffering, and this path did not lead him back to his wife, but away from her and indeed away from all women. For the essence of wisdom among all his faithful male followers was to remain celibate and to shun the pleasures of the flesh and the temptations which women place before men and which place men in bondage. Buddha never returned to his wife. Even today, the Buddhist Nirvana does not include women.

Judaism and Women

Judaism also has a rich patriarchal tradition, beginning with Genesis: "And God said, Let us make *man* [not woman] in our image, after our likeness; and let them [not women] have dominion over the fish of the sea, and over the fowl of the air, and over the cattle, and over all the earth, and over every creeping thing that creepeth upon the earth." (Gen. 1:1)

"Unto the woman He said, I will greatly multiply thy sorrow, and thy conception; in sorrow thou shalt bring forth children; and thy desire shall be to thy husband, and he shall *rule* over thee." (Gen. 3:16)

THE LOCKHORNS

"I'M NOT STARTING AN ARGUMENT! THIS IS THE SAME ONE YOU STARTED YESTERDAY!"

The Ten Comandments, as given to Moses, addressed themselves clearly to male-female relations, and it is plain that their intent is to bring wives under the rule of their husbands, and children under the rule of their parents.

"Honor thy father and thy mother: that thy days may be long upon the land which the Lord thy God giveth thee." (Exod. 20:12) "Thou shalt not commit adultery." (Exod. 20:14) "Thou shalt not covet thy neighbor's wife." (Exod. 20:12)

The same fellow who wrote Proverbs 21:19—"It is better to dwell in the wilderness than with a contentious and angry woman"—probably also wrote Proverbs 21:9—"It is better to dwell in a corner of the housetop than with a brawling woman in a wide house." Perhaps he also wrote Proverbs 9:13—"A foolish woman is clamorous; she is simple, and knoweth nothing." Proverbs 7:11—"She is loud and stubborn; her feet abide not in her house." Proverbs 27:15—"A continual dropping on a very rainy day and a contentious woman are alike." Proverbs 14:1—"The wisest women build up their homes." Proverbs 1:20—"A foolish woman raises her voice in public places." Proverbs 7:11-12—"She is loud and wayward, now in the street, now in the market, lying in wait at every corner." Proverbs 21:25—"A good wife is clothed in dignity and power, and can afford to laugh at tomorrow." (Compare this to the old Lebanese proverb: Better to eat camel dung alone than to share honey with the whole tribe.)

Listen to the lamentations of Isaiah (beloved of Jesus) regarding the plight of a crumbling Israel:

"For behold, the Lord, the Lord of hosts, doth take away from Jerusalem and from Judah the stay and the staff, the whole stay of bread, and the whole stay of water,

"The mighty man, and the man of war, the judge, and the prophet, and the prudent and the ancient,

"The captain of fifty, and the honorable man, and the

counsellor, and the cunning artificer, and the eloquent orator.

"And I will give children to be their princes, and babes shall rule over them.

"And the people shall be oppressed, every one by another, and every one by his neighbor: *the child shall behave himself proudly against the ancient*, and the base against the honorable . . .

"For Jerusalem is ruined, and Judah is fallen; because their tongue and their doings are against the Lord . . ." (Isa. 3:1-8)

"As for my people, children are their oppressors, and women rule over them." (Isa. 3:12)

Isaiah, like so many of the prophets who preceded and followed him, was unnerved by the haughty daughters of Zion and prophesied that they would meet a terrible fate—madness, sickness, and early death. There is an immediacy about his words which suggests that he, too, had had experience with the Zeldas and Kilgallens of his times:

"Moreover, the Lord saith, Because the daughters of Zion are haughty, and walk with stretched-forth necks and wanton eyes, walking and mincing as they go, and making a tinkling with their feet;

"Therefore the Lord will smite with a scab the crown of the head of the daughters of Zion, and the Lord will discover their secret parts.

"In that day the Lord will take away the bravery of their tinkling ornaments about their feet, and their cauls, and their round tires like the moon,

"The chains, and the bracelets, and the mufflers,

"The bonnets, and the ornaments of the legs, and the headbands, and the tablets, and the earrings,

"The rings, and nose jewels,

"The changeable suits of apparel, and the mantles, and the wimples, and the crisping pins,

"The glasses, and the fine linen, and the hoods, and the vails.

"And it shall come to pass that instead of sweet smell there shall be stink; and instead of a girdle a rent; and instead of well-set hair baldness; and instead of a stomacher a girding of sackcloth; and burning instead of beauty.

"Thy men shall fall by the sword, and thy mighty in the war.

"And her gates shall lament and mourn; and she being desolate shall sit upon the ground."

THE LOCKHORNS

"YEAH? WELL, IF YOU <u>COULD</u> HAVE MARRIED A BETTER MAN, I CAN GUARANTEE HE WOULDN'T BE A BETTER MAN BY NOW!"

Note that Isaiah mentions, in the same breath, the haughty women of Zion, war, and the devastation of Israel. Like those before him, he clearly saw the relationship between feminists, violence, and war.

The Talmud says that "a daughter is a vain treasure to her

father. From anxiety about her he does not sleep at night; during her early years, lest she be seduced; in her adolescence, lest she go astray; in her marriageable years, lest she does not find a husband; when she is married, lest she be childless; and when she is old, lest she practice witchcraft." Says a Jewish prayer, "I thank Thee, Lord, that Thou has not created me a woman." The Messiah that the Jews have always looked for was never a woman.

Christianity and Women

Christianity took its patriarchal tradition and its view of women as troublemakers from Judaism. In fact, Jesus Christ came at a time that was similar to that which Isaiah laments. The women and children of Israel were running wild; madness, violence, war, and sickness plagued the land; families were being torn asunder by conflicts between fathers and mothers, parents and children; robbers, bandits, and criminals roamed the land at will; women exerted great influence in political councils; and the synagogues of Israel had become, by and large, feminized, with the rabbis and high priests deferring to the advice of their female parishioners and giving them all their hearts desired. In short, Israel was ruled by her women and her children, as Isaiah had prophesied, and her men were at war with one another.

Early Christianity was a decidedly masculinist movement, just as Judaism had been earlier. All of Christ's apostles were men. He never chose a woman to be a disciple. Nor did Christ set himself at odds with the Jewish patriarchal tradition. "Think not that I am come to destroy the law, or the prophets; I am not come to destroy, but to fulfill." (Matt. 5:17) That is, he had come, among other things, to restore man to the head of his household, to be master over his wife and children. "Blessed are the peacemakers, for they shall be called the children of God." (Matt. 5:9)

Christ was a healer, as well as a peacemaker, and it is clear that he, like Isaiah and the psychiatrists of today, was keenly aware of the sickness and madness that family strife invariably generates: "And the children shall rise up against their parents, and cause them to be put to death." (Matt. 11:21) "And a man's foes shall be they of his own household." (Matt. 11:36) "Every house divided against itself shall not stand." (Matt. 12:25)

It was clear to Jesus' disciples that while their master commanded men to be humble before God, he expected women to be humble before men. St. Mark tells us of Jesus' appreciation of a woman's act of pouring ointment on his head in the house of Simon the leper in Bethany. As he sat at meat, reports St. Mark (14:3), a woman came in carrying an alabaster box of ointment of spikenard. She broke the box and poured the precious ointment over Jesus' head. Some of the disciples were indignant, but Jesus said, "Let her alone; why trouble ye her? She hath wrought a good work on me."

Did Jesus, like Isaiah, have the haughty daughters of Zion in mind when he said, "Whosoever shall exalt himself shall be abased; and he that shall humble himself shall be exalted"? (Matt. 23:12) Was it possible that Jesus also intended to exalt woman by humbling her?

Jesus was not antiwoman, but he was antifeminist. To be sure, his commandments to the men of Israel, as well as to the women, were plainly meant to preserve the family and to give women some protection from the wanderlust of men. It is clear in the accounts of all four apostles and St. Paul that the question of divorce was a burning issue in Jesus' time, as it is today. It is mentioned frequently in the New Testament, and Jesus' answer to it saddened his disciples then, as much as it does now. For then, as well as now, Christ's disciples, though reluctant to give up their riches and worldly possessions to follow Jesus, seemed to be delighted by the idea of giving up their wives to take up the cross.

Jesus' answer greatly distressed them. "And I say unto you, Whosoever shall put away his wife, except it be for fornication, and shall marry another, committeth adultery: and whoso marrieth her which is put away doth commit adultery." (Matt. 19:9) His disciples responded, we are told, by saying to Jesus, "If the case of the man be so with his wife, it is not good to marry."

The reaction of the disciples to Jesus' commandment tells us a good deal about the times. The institution of marriage had apparently become so shaky, turbulent, and hellish that the disciples concluded that it was better not to go into it if one were not able to get out of it. From this passage developed the monastic tradition in Christianity.

The Reverend Dr. William E. Phipps of Elkins, West Virginia, has just published a book called *Was Jesus Married?* in which he speculated that Jesus was indeed. Reverend Phipps notes that scholars have examined every aspect of Jesus' life except the question of his marital status. "This absence is especially enigmatic," says Phipps, "since marriage was the one social institution that Jesus blessed and used in his parables to illustrate the Gospel. Jesus, according to John, first "manifested his glory" at a wedding feast at Cana, producing 150 gallons of wine for the wedding party.

Reverend Phipps speculates that Jesus may have either been widowed or divorced. Knowing what we know about Buddha's, Mohammed's, and Tolstoy's turbulent marriages (which preceded their religious awakenings), it is not altogether impossible that Jesus as a youth was also married to a shrew who made his life a daily torment.

On the other hand, there is no evidence to suggest, as it has become fashionable to suggest, that Jesus was homosexual. Nicholas Benton, cofounder of the Gay Student Union at the Pacific School of Religion, contends that "we have no reason to believe that Jesus was 'straight.' " Benton urges the church to abandon its historical opposition to homosexuality. He claims that today "homosexuality is rampant among ministers and seminarians."

In point of fact, the early Christians, as did the Jews before them and the Moslems after them, damned homosexuality. Tertullian, though an antifeminist, notes, "So far as sex is concerned, the Christian is content with the woman." There is nothing in Jesus' teachings which sanctions homosexuality. Indeed, it is more likely that Jesus regarded homosexuality as a condition, a state of mind like other states of mind, from which a man could escape if he denied himself and followed Him. Jesus would have found beauty in the love of a man for another man, but not in the lust of a man for another man. It is asking us too much to believe that a prophet, the thrust of whose teachings was aimed at preserving the family, would sanction a practice which is today breaking up many families, as it probably was doing in His days.

Perhaps Jesus' observations and instructions regarding male-female relationships explain, as well as anything else does, why he was finally crucified. The New Testament is silent on the role the influential feminists of Israel, the girl friends of the Pharisees, and the wives of the Roman rulers may have played in stirring up public support for Jesus' crucifixion. But we can be sure that they were not passive observers. Remember, it was Salome who had John the Baptist beheaded, an event that greatly saddened Jesus. Indeed, St. Matthew suggests that, while Pontius Pilate himself seemed to be rather favorably disposed toward Jesus, his wife was not. "When he [Pontius Pilate] was set down on the judgment seat, his wife sent unto him, saying, Have thou nothing to do with that just man: for I have suffered many things this day in a dream because of him." (Matt. 27:19) This is, of course, open to two interpretations, but it is not improbable that Pilate's wife, offended by the masculinist teachings of Jesus, urged her husband to destroy this impudent man. Further biblical and historical research may one day establish the fact that the feminists of Israel and the wives and girl friends of the Pharisees and the Romans had more to do with the crucifixion than is generally supposed. The chances are good they were right there howling for blood along with everyone else.

Indeed, it has been written that Tertullian of Carthage, an early Christian father, was declaring that women are "the gate by which the demon enters" about the same time that Mani of Ctesiphon, a young Persian mystic, was insisting that "woman is Satan's masterpiece." Tertullian also once told an assembly of women that "it is on your account that Jesus Christ died."

God became incarnate in a man, not a woman, and was crucified.

The tradition of male hegemony is deeply rooted among Christians. "Let your women keep silence in the churches, for it is not permitted unto them to speak; but they are commanded to be under obedience, as also saith the law," declared St. Paul (I Cor. 14:34-35). "And if they will learn anything, let them ask their husbands at home: for it is a shame for women to speak in the church."

Again, Paul: "For the man is not of the woman; but the woman of the man. Neither was the man created for the woman; but the woman for the man." (I Cor. 11:3-9)

THE LOCKHORNS

"I KNOW YOU'RE LISTENING. I CAN HEAR YOU GRINDING YOUR TEETH!"

"Let the women learn in silence with all subjection. But I suffer not a woman to teach, nor to usurp authority over the man, but to be in silence. For Adam was first formed, then Eve. And Adam was not deceived, but the woman being deceived was in the transgression." (I Tim. 2:11-14)

"Wives, submit yourselves unto your own husbands, as unto the Lord. For the husband is the head of the wife, even as Christ is the head of the Church; and he is the Saviour of the body. Therefore, as the Church is subject unto Christ, so let the wives be to their own husbands in every thing." (Eph. 5:22-24)

"Husbands, love your wives, even as Christ also loved the Church, and gave himself for it. He that loveth his wife loveth himself." (Eph. 5:25-29)

The foregoing advice makes it readily understandable why St. Paul was often in jail, suffered all manner of persecution, and was almost always on the move from city to city. People could put up with blasphemy and the authorities might even put up with cries for revolution, but no one could tolerate for long a madman who advised wives to be obedient to their husbands, and husbands to love and not to divorce their wives. It also explains why Paul was such a prolific letter writer. It is safer to write such advice than to deliver it in person.

What is significant is the unanimity of the disciples on the question of male supremacy. The disciples raised many doubts and questions in the presence of their master, but none, not even the doubting Thomas, doubted the wisdom of the husband headship principle. Peter echoed Paul: "Likewise ye wives, be in subjection to your own husbands." (I Peter 3:1)

Both Jesus and Paul suggested that it was difficult for a man to get into the kingdom of heaven if he were married. Paul was a bit ambivalent on this point. To some, he advised that it was better to marry than to burn. To others, he advised that those who marry were more likely to burn than those who didn't. And Paul's ambivalence on the issue has carried over into the life of the Church even today. In the early centuries of Christianity, clerical celibacy was more the exception than the rule, the Church fathers notwithstanding.

Clement of Alexandria, a third-century Church father, contended that marriage contributed to salvation. Nevertheless, a thousand years of experience to the contrary inspired the Second Lateran Council in 1139 to make celibacy obligatory for all clergy. Recently a group of Catholic priests formed the National Association for Pastoral Renewal with the intention of fighting mandatory celibacy. However, it is our understanding that the group is now having trouble attracting supporters, or so says Robert Duggan, a priest who married and who heads the association. After an initial outburst of enthusiasm for the idea of matrimony, a lot of priests are backing off now. Most of them have listened too long to the tales of marital woe in the confessionals to be deluded into supposing that marriage is the path to salvation, when many of their parishioners are daily avowing that it is, in fact, the path to hell.

The anger of the gentle St. Francis was roused on only one point. The Franciscans were a lay Catholic movement at the beginning, and his was also a masculinist movement. St. Francis, according to Nikos Kazantzakis, worried about the possibility of women joining and disrupting his movement. He declined the requests of women to join the Franciscans, fearing the trouble that comes with the mixing of the sexes.

Probably the biggest mistake the Catholic church has made was canonizing Joan of Arc. It may be argued that most of the church's troubles date from the time that the Maid of Orleans was declared a saint. The church hasn't been the same since. Joan's Inquisitors had recognized her for what she was—an arrogant, hallucinating, bloodthirsty witch disguised as a warrior, who had the effrontery to challenge not only the English armies but also the patriarchal authority of the church, and they could not forgive her for that. So they burned her. Joan carried all of France to war with her, and for that the church, bowing to feminist pressure, was later to make her a saint. In so doing, the church in effect gave its blessings to all of the feminists yet to come, and opened a Pandora's box.

The Protestant movement developed as a direct result of the increasing feminization of the Catholic church, which had begun to make saints of women in violation of St. Paul's and St. Peter's strictures. Again in history, the feminization of a religious institution and its subsequent decline resulted in the spinning off of new sects which claimed that the parent institution had betrayed its original principles. Martin Luther, John Calvin, and John Knox challenged the authority and practices of the Catholic church on numerous points. But of special importance is the fact that they all insisted on continuing the patriarchal tradition in the Lutheran and Presbyterian churches. "Woman, in her greatest perfection, was made to serve and obey man," declared Knox.

John Wesley had no illusions about women or the matrimonial state. Church historians record that Wesley had as difficult a wife as a man was ever cursed with. To get away from her, Wesley was forever on the road evangelizing, as much for his own sanity as for Christ. It has been said that, had Wesley not been unhappily married, the Methodist church would never have been formed and spread as fast as it did. But perhaps the major reason Methodism captured the imagination and hearts of so many in England and later in America is that Wesley preached with great ardor what Christ and Paul had preached, commanding women to honor and obey their husbands.

The patriarchal tradition in Christianity was carried over in most of the breakaway Protestant sects, with the exception of the Christian Scientists, who accepted Mary Baker Eddy as a spokesman for Christ, and the Seventh-Day Adventists, founded by Ellen White. It should be noted that both Mary

Baker Eddy and Ellen White suffered themselves from a variety of chronic mental and physical ailments. Both suffered from repeated attacks of hysteria, according to objective biographers, and Ellen White often slipped into trances while preaching from the pulpit. Both had much of value to say. Both restated the eternal mental and physiological verities relating to health and sickness which Christ had declared in his ministry of healing. But they made a fetish of health, and incorporated into their systems only those of Christ's and Paul's commandments which did not conflict with their militant feminism.

THE LOCKHORNS

"YOU FOOL, YOU! YOU BLOODY FOOL!"

Christian Science is, in some respects, perhaps the major heresy of Christianity. It exalted the feminists and equated Mary Baker Eddy's mind with Jesus Christ's. To Mary Baker Eddy, there was only one "Mind," neither masculine nor feminine, and she exhorted many Christian Science ladies "to take on the mind of Christ," a very powerful and masculine mind indeed. They were exhorted, too, to flout the patriarchal tradition of the Church.

What neither Mary Baker Eddy nor Ellen White understood was what Moses, Isaiah, Christ, Peter, Paul, St. Francis, John Knox, and Wesley had seen all too clearly—the enormous amount of sickness, madness, and social disorder that is generated by a family at war with itself, by husband-and-wife and male-and-female conflicts. The prophets' aim was to bring peace to the family. The net effect, if not the intention, of Christian Science and the Seventh-Day Adventist movement was to bring a sword to the family.

Mary Baker Eddy herself was married, three times, and was unable to make any one of her husbands happy. Her third husband died of heart disease, which did not exist only in his mind. Her only son disliked her intensely. Ellen White never succeeded in rising above her lifelong trances and attacks of hysteria, and was not a happy woman at her death. Divorce and illness are not uncommon today, even among Christian Science practitioners, and if an objective statistical study were possible, it is likely to be found that they suffer from precisely the same ailments as the rest of the matriarchal population.

Freud and Mary Baker Eddy are philosophical first cousins. Both of their movements are a direct outgrowth of the feminist movement.

Islam and Women

The prophet Mohammed appeared at a time which rather strikingly resembles the present in the United States. The women of pagan Arabia were running wild and had achieved great power. The Arabian tribes were warring and bickering among themselves, and the entire countryside was torn by strife, banditry, madness, and social disorder. Some of the tribes worshipped goddesses not dissimilar to Mary Baker Eddy and Ellen White, and built temples for them. This was one of Mohammed's chief complaints. He was especially vexed that the Meccans were worshipping the three goddesses—Manat, Allat, and Al'Uzza.

The prophet's reply to the goddess-worshippers is dramatically recorded in the Koran: "What? Shall Allah have daughters and not sons?" one translation has it. Another version has Mohammed saying, "What? Shall ye have male progeny and Allah female? This were indeed an unfair partition."

THE LOCKHORNS

"WELL, WITH PROPER CARE YOU SHOULD GET ANOTHER FIFTEEN MILLION WORDS OUT OF IT."

In another passage, the Koran declares: "Yet they assign to Him offspring from among his servants! Surely man is monstrously ungrateful. Would Allah choose daughters for Himself and sons for you? Yet when the birth of a daughter is announced to one of them, his face darkens and is filled with gloom. Would they ascribe to Allah females who adorn themselves in trinkets and are powerless in disputation?"

Not much is known about Mohammed's life prior to his emergence as the prophet who transformed Arabia. A merchant, he was married to a woman older than he. He subsequently suffered what appears to have been a nervous breakdown, and retreated to the caves in the desert to fast and pray. We can only guess what his relations were with his wife, but judging by the writings of Buddha, Wesley, Tolstoy, and others who turned to religion after cracking up under the strain of living with their contentious wives, we may safely assume that Mohammed's relations with his wife were less than idyllic.

The fact that Mohammed, like Christ and Moses before him, emerged from the desert preaching a fiery masculinist religion suggests that Islam may have been in part shaped by Mohammed's earlier, pagan relationship with his wife. It is no coincidence that he reserved his sharpest words for the goddesses and those male collaborators who insisted on putting them on pedestals. Also, while Mohammed went into the desert from a state of monogamy, he came out of the desert preaching polygamy. He himself subsequently had several wives, an indication that he may have come to the conclusion that there is indeed safety in numbers. (Other students of Islam have suggested that the reason the Prophet allowed his followers each to take four wives is because intertribal warfare in pre-Islamic, matriarchal Arabia had so decimated the country's manhood that there was a short supply of men and far too many eligible women, whom Mohammed wished to rescue from prostitution, begging, and neurosis.)

Evidently, the women of Arabia were mesmerized by this man. They loved him. Women generally like homosexuals, but they love prophets. While homosexuals in all times have run away from woman, the prophets of all times have met her head-on and humbled her. And that is why women, as a rule, prefer prophets to homosexuals.

Mohammed restored the Arab male to the head of his family, restored his sense of dignity and pride in his manhood, returned law and order, grace, courtesy, chivalry, and hospitality to the life of Arabia. He gave all authority to the Moslim male over his wife and children. He gave the male the power to put away his wife if she did not please him, and all he had to do was to utter the words "I divorce thee" three times, and no man would have anything to do with that disgraced woman thereafter.

Mohammed also understood the sexual problems which arise when women rule over men. An old Arab proverb, derived from the Islamic tradition, declares: Woman who treat husband like servant all day cannot expect him to act like king in bed at night.

Ja'far Ibn-Abi-Talib, an early Moslem spokesman, has written: "Jahilyah [ignorant] people were we, worshipping idols, feeding on dead animals, deserting our families, with the strong among us devouring the weak. Such was our state until Allah sent unto us a messenger from amongst ourselves. He commanded us to stand by our families; he forbade committing fornication and speaking ill of chaste women . . ." Arab historian Philip K. Hitti confirms that the Arabian family organization was matriarchal before the arrival of Mohammed.

Arabic poetry, too, either waxes romantically about women or bewails the many troubles that come in their wake. In his *Luzumiyat*, the poet Abu'l-Ala-Ma'arri laments the death of his wife thusly with this epitaph:

> Beneath this stone
> my wife doth lie
> now she's at peace
> and so am I

To the present day, Arabic versifiers blame all misfortunes on Al-Manaya (Manat), the goddess of destiny, and one of the three goddesses whom the pagan Arabians of Mecca and Medina worshipped prior to the arrival of Mohammed. But Mohammed was also solicitous of women: "Ye people!" the prophet declared in one of his last speeches in Mecca, "Ye have rights demandable of your wives, and they have rights demandable of you. Upon them it is incumbent not to violate their conjugal faith nor commit any act of impropriety. Treat your women well!" Today in Moslem countries, though the legal status of women is not good according to Western standards, one would still be hard put to find a Moslem boy who hates his mother. One is courting certain death if one insults a Moslem's mother, wife, or sister.

Just as Judaism was a masculinist response to the madness and chaos that had accompanied the feminization of the earlier institutions of the Israelis, and just as Christianity was a masculinist response to the feminization of Judaism, Islam was a masculinist response to the feminization of Christianity and the pagan religions of Arabia. Women were not even allowed to set foot in a mosque, since their presence would defile a holy place.

Historians have often wondered what gave Islam its special power and appeal, but these were no greater than the power and appeal of Judaism and Christianity at their earliest, masculinist beginnings. It was only when the institutions of these religions fell later under the influence of the feminists and their collaborators that they began to lose their appeal to the masses. This, more than anything else, explains the rise and fall, the ebb and flow of all religious institutions.

Consider the Koran's instructions to good Moslim men regarding their wives, and one can readily understand why Arab males, young and old, rich and poor, merchant and camel-driver, sheik and servant, rallied enthusiastically—nay, fervently—to Mohammed's cause:

"Men have authority over women because Allah has made the one superior to the other, and because they spend their wealth to maintain them. Good women are obedient. As for those from whom you fear disobedience, admonish them and send them to beds apart and beat them. Then if they obey you, take no further action against them. Allah is High, Supreme."

Add to this the fact that the Koran, in several passages, promises every good and faithful Moslim male eternal life in a paradise populated by beautiful virgins endlessly waiting on him.

Now perhaps it may be clear why Islam swept across several continents, all the way to Spain to the west and to India and Ceylon to the east. It may now also be clear why the Black Muslims have won the hearts and loyalty of a large segment of the black community in matriarchal America, and why Islam is by far the fastest growing religion in Africa today. Not long ago, Cassius Clay, a Black Muslim, came to Ann Arbor and addressed a crowd at the University of Michigan. He got the most applause—thunderous, in fact— when he declared, "Women ain't supposed to be equal."

As we have seen, all of the great religions shared a distrust of women. All of them attempted to elevate the male to the head of the family. All of them attempted to exalt the female by humbling her. All of them believed in witchcraft. And at the heart of every religion is the word "peace": "shalom," "Prince of Peace," "Islam." All of the prophets of every religion were convinced that there could be no such thing as peace in the world without peace in the home. ("And a man's foes shall be they of his own household.") And all of them understood that there can be no peace, security, safety, or respect for women in a society that does not respect its manhood.

THE LOCKHORNS

"LEROY! HE WAS PLAYING OUR SONG!"

All of them regarded the male and female roles as sacred, to be violated at the risk of one's sanity, health, and happiness. And all of them insisted on consecrating the marital relationship with a priest or holy man performing the marriage rite.

The times in America today are eerily similar to the conditions which preceded the emergence of the great male avatars. There are many other signs that we are undergoing "the last days" described by Isaiah. Not only are we worshipping goddesses like Mary Baker Eddy, Ellen White, and Aimee Semple McPherson, but our women and our children are ruling and oppressing us in our homes, in our schools, in our churches, in our governments, in our courts, and in our offices. Our laws are being written by women, and they are writing them in their own favor. Whereas the laws in all sane and civilized societies have been aimed at preserving the family, even at the cost of subjugating the female, America's laws today in regard to divorce, alimony, child custody, and equal employment opportunities for women conspire toward the destruction of the family.

We have arrived at those last days when, as Jesus tells us, "a man's foes shall be they of his own household." Here is another sign: Not long ago, the Episcopal church experimented with a new liturgy which required churchgoers, at the end of a service, to take the hand of the person sitting next to them in the pew and to speak kind and neighborly words to him or her. A great resentment suddenly developed toward the new liturgy, and church officials, searching for the reasons, conducted a study and found that it was more difficult for husbands and wives to enter into friendly after-service communication than it was for strangers.

Still another sign: the divorce rate among the clergy is almost as high as the divorce rate among the rest of the population. Ministers are seemingly having as much trouble with their wives as lay people, as the patriarchal traditions of the church continue to crumble.

Women have, by and large, taken over most of the nation's

churches, with the possible exceptions of the Catholic and Orthodox churches. In most Protestant denominations, women can now be ordained as ministers. The president of the National Council of Churches is a woman. Women, in fact, make up a majority of the membership of most churches. Women's caucuses have been formed in virtually every major denomination, and they are demonstrating and demanding more power. Even militant nuns are challenging the patriarchal authority of the church. Priests are marrying and falling under the spell of militant feminists, and an increasing number of them are supporting the strident demands of the Women's Liberationists. Divorce, though unsanctioned by the church, is increasing among Catholics.

To a large extent, the churches of America have already been feminized, and we can expect that in the near future, they will be even more so. History teaches us that whenever the religious institutions of a society are feminized, they begin to lose their influence among the masses. The society then degenerates into chaos. If the society is lucky, the religious institution is then reformed by a masculinist movement from within (take the example of the Franciscans of the twelfth century, inspired by God's command to St. Francis of Assisi to "Go hence and build up My House, for it is falling down!")

Or, a new, fiercely masculinist religion arises, with a new prophet, to challenge the older, feminized religion.

Samra's Footnote
and Samra's Prophecy

The Male Liberators and the
Attempt to Regain Control

There are already several hopeful signs that the American male is beginning to rebel against the matriarchy in which he lives, develops nerves like tattered dishrags, and dies an early death. The Black Muslims have emerged as a significant force within the black community. Both men and women are beginning to question the wisdom of the feminist movement. And masculinist divorce-reform and law-reform organizations are proliferating throughout the country, though they have not yet received a fraction of the attention or publicity the feminist groups have received. Recently, U.S. divorce-reform organizations appealed to the United Nations to rescue the beleaguered American male. (A list of masculinist organizations may be found in the appendix.)

"If this feminist thing is allowed to continue unchallenged," one masculinist warned recently, "they shall end by making faggots or Muslims of us all."

Some of the men in the masculinist groups see in the indifference of the press to their cause a conspiracy of silence nurtured by what they privately speak of as the feminestablishment. The feminestablishment, they maintain, runs everything in America behind the scenes—the press, the federal government, the arts, book publishing, Hollywood, etc. Its influence reaches into the higher councils of government, and sometimes strange things happen to those who dare to criticize publicly the tenets upon which the movement is based.

The Feminestablishment

Does the feminestablishment really exist, or is it a figment of the imagination of desperate men? There is conflicting information as regards this point, but one masculinist writer who has for years vainly sought a publisher who would publish his manuscript, cites the following report from Marylin Bender, writing in *The New York Times Book Review*, as proof of the feminestablishment's existence:

"Isn't it ironic that the book publishing industry which has always underpaid, underrated, and underemployed the second sex, should now be gallantly courting the Women's Liberation Movement? Almost every major publisher either has a feminist under contract or wishes he did . . . The interest in the latest drive for total female equality is like the panic that hit publishing six or seven years ago when everyone was tripping over each other to get a black list . . . The book publishers' hunch that feminism may be the dominant social movement of the seventies ('the next two big revolutions are going to be women and then homosexuals,' says Coward-McCann's Ellis Amburn) follows a spate of newspaper and magazine articles . . . Certainly, the immediate future holds a scramble for contracts and an assortment of quickie projects."

THE LOCKHORNS

"BUT ENOUGH ABOUT MY TROUBLES···
HOW IS YOUR HUSBAND?"

But when 150 members of the American Society for Divorced Men picketed the Civic Center Plaza in Chicago on October 18, 1970, to protest alleged discrimination against males in the American divorce process, *The New York Times*, which had been giving the feminists front-page treatment for months, noted the men's action in a one-paragraph item buried on the bottom of page 65.

So difficult has it been for masculinists to penetrate publishing circles with their tracts and books, that one male liberator began writing under the pen name M. Ann Evans, in the hopes of being published. "M. Ann Evans" is in fact Jay Burchett, a professor of engineering and technology at a western college, who is one of the founders of United States Divorce Reform, Inc. "M. Ann Evans" is listed as the editor of the *Law Reform Review*, a lively newsletter published by the Family Education & Information Council of the United States in Corona Del Mar, California, and he is forever blasting away at the injustices of the divorce court system.

Mr. Burchett is, of course, frequently asked why he writes under the pen name M. Ann Evans. Reason: in the nineteenth century the novelist Mary Ann Evans (1814-1880), having had much difficulty getting her work accepted by publishers because she was a woman, decided to take the pen name George Eliot. She immediately prospered. Burchett believes that things have come full circle, and male authors are now being discriminated against. Thus, just as Mary Ann Evans became George Eliot in order to be published, Jay Burchett has become M. Ann Evans in order to be published.

Burchett is tough, relentless, and courageous in the face of great odds. He is a male liberator, the forerunner of the New Man. Another brave and spirited man molded in much the same tradition is Earl Nicholas Kurtz who, like Burchett, comes to the movement by way of a divorce.

E. N. Kurtz and the He-Man's Message Association

Few persons have ever heard of Earl Nicholas Kurtz. Kurtz is eighty-two and lives in Columbia, Missouri. For most of his life, he has been trying to alert America to the dangers of feminism. He believes that the salvation of the world lies in woman's return to children and kitchen, and that it was a "master-stroke of imbecility" to give women the vote. A prolific writer, Kurtz has written over four hundred essays on the subject of women, most of which he had to mimeograph himself for want of a media outlet for his writings.

In 1930, not long after women were given the vote, Kurtz formed the He-Man's Message Association and put out his first—and as it turned out, his last—newsletter, called *The Male Voice*. The aim of the organization, which also did not survive, was surprisingly similar to SEAM's—"the restitution of Patriarchal Government where the Father is the Head of the Home." The organization was "founded upon the faith that, as men and women differ physically, so do they differ mentally, which of necessity proves that any woman who makes a good mother naturally makes a poor father, or vice versa."

In an article in the newsletter titled "The Hand That Rules the Cradle Rocks the World," Kurtz declared:

"The first law ever given a human being was given to the first transgressor—the woman: 'Thy husband shall rule over thee.' (Gen. 3:16), but the nineteenth amendment of the Constitution of this great country says in effect: 'Your husband shall not rule over thee; you are free.' Hence we reap what we have sown.

"Men are losing respect for women because women have lost respect for themselves. Man cannot and will not protect and provide for his own equal; hence, fifty-fifty-ism is wrong.

"When the word 'obey' was omitted from the marriage ceremony, it turned the home—which is the foundation of all civilization—over to a committee of two, and since a committee of two cannot get a majority vote, chaos and lawlessness reign supreme, because our home life is broken down . . .

"It was the church that eliminated the word 'obey' from the holy marriage vow and put over Woman Suffrage, thereby fostering the lack of respect and confidence which is so generally and righteously manifested toward the church at present . . . The slogan of the feminist was, 'we will gain control of the church first and then we will take charge of the state.' This they have done . . .

THE LOCKHORNS

12-19

'COME IN, DEAR·····WE WERE JUST
TALKING ABOUT YOU!"

"The brunt of all the social disturbances of today is the rebellion of the wife. Satan puts it in the hearts of women to rebel against man and also the desire to rule him, thus reversing the order as originally intended. This militant tyranny never materialized until feminism reduced the time-old ideals of the church to a flagrant vulgarity . . .

'But I would have you know that the head of every man is Christ; and the head of every woman is the man; and the head of Christ is God.' (I Cor. 11:7) What Christ is to man,

man is to woman. There is but one right way, and if our ancestors practiced holy matrimony thru, 'Love, Honor and Obey,' then all other matrimony is unholy . . ." He adds: "As God is our Father, not Mother, so Christ was a man and not a woman."

The "satanic agencies" responsible for the spread of feminism and its attendant chaos, Kurtz claims, are the organized church and Bolshevism. Kurtz, incidentally, comes from a long line of ministers and scholars.

Kurtz gives the following explanation of the source of female power: "When the master falls in love with the pupil, the pupil becomes the master."

Mr. Kurtz's views have not changed in forty years, but indeed have been strengthened, he says. He still insists we must restore the "headship" principle to man, and he still likes to use the world "Eve-ill." ("The first Adam HEAR-kened unto the 'Voice' of his wife. That got us out of Eden.") He points out that Christ's whole "theme-song" was "fatherhood headship."

Even today Kurtz hasn't stopped fighting the good fight. Recently he wrote SEAM, offering "to coordinate our respec-tive positions to a united power-effort for a better world . . . Your approach is to DO something FOR men—primarily; whereas I contend that man—the new man—or better-man to a better world—is by destiny, due to DO something as regards his 'self.' Christ was only the first-fruits—a better male to eventually raise the entire status of the herd or flock."

The Phon E. Hudkins Report

Still another male liberator is Phon E. Hudkins (the name is for real.) In April, 1970, Hudkins, a Labor Department economist-lawyer, unnerved his superiors when he issued a two-hundred-page report blaming women for most of men's ailments and favoring the repeal of the sex provision of the Civil Rights Act. The act aims at equal job opportunities and equal pay for women. The Labor Department immediately disclaimed any connection with the Hudkins report.

Hudkins, a slight, balding bachelor of thirty-six who lives in Washington, pointed out that the 1968 Manpower Report stressed that "family stability should be a primary objective of manpower policy." He maintained that studies on riots, crime, delinquency, divorce, suicide, homosexuality, alcoholism, paranoia, and schizophrenia all point to the same cause: disorganized homes, a breakdown of family structure, a lack of male dominance.

Hudkins presented statistics showing that the Negro family especially is "in deep trouble," and that the composition of the black family "is becoming more and more female-dominated." Female heads of nonwhite families, he said, are becoming more the common rule. "At present, 1.2 million black low-income youths (three-fourths of all black children in city families with income under $4,000) are living in *fatherless* homes," Hudkins said. He agreed with the conclusion of two black psychiatrists, who wrote in the book *Black Rage*, that "a great many of the problems of black people in America can be traced back to the widespread crumbling of the family structure . . ."

(*Life* magazine recently did a report on mixed dating, and found that "young black men and women have a serious problem relating to one another, partly because black women are fatally ready to snipe at black men." A passage from the report: "The black (female) personality professor acknowledges the problem: 'Wow, our mouth. We'll use that tongue on you, cut you to pieces. We really will. At the same time we're digging you and loving you all the while.' The new black man has little patience with his woman's scalding tongue. 'I wouldn't go out with one of those nigger bitches for all the money in the world. They're mean, they're evil, they're hard to get along with,' snarls a black graduate student who dates white women exclusively. Another says: 'It's time black women were busted back where they belong.' " The article quotes one black woman as saying: "Progress for us is going to have to start with the improvement of the black male-female relationship." That is precisely what the Black Muslims are trying to do, with considerable success, but *Life* pointedly ignored that phenomenon.)

Said Hudkins about both blacks and whites: "We find that manpower policies are causing these physical and mental illnesses in the long run. Many men are trapped in low-income jobs. If we are going to make males the head of the family, they have to have jobs."

And yet, Hudkins noted, "many of our manpower training programs have enrolled larger numbers of females." He urged a dramatic change in the nation's manpower policies and practices, including:

1) Repeal of the sex provision of the Civil Rights Act. "Men must be given the first opportunities for vocational preparation and for job opportunities."

2) Manpower development and training activities must be redirected toward males—especially youth. "If males are to serve their primary function—the protection of their family—they must be given priority in upgrading of their employment and must be given top security in their jobs so their families can rely on them."

3) Males should be guaranteed a job which will enable them to support their families. "The government should prepare now to be the employer of last resort to all *males* affected by a slowdown in the economy."

4) Vocational education should be redirected toward males.

5) The overall mission of manpower policy should include all males—poor and nonpoor, black and white. "The overriding goal of manpower policy should be to give every male the continuous opportunity for suitable employment in a job where he can utilize his full productive potential for his own and for society's benefit."

6) The centers of implementation of training and compensatory education programs should be reasonably small in size and include males only.

7) Welfare programs should be changed to encourage the male to be the head of the family. "From an economic standpoint, AFDC, as currently administered, provides a subsidy for separation."

8) Government programs for the disadvantaged should be run by men so that the disadvantaged male has a role model to identify with. "Placing young men under dominant women will only increase their long-run psychological disabilities."

Other Labor Department officials have, privately to be sure, expressed alarm that women are increasingly displacing men on the labor market. According to the most recent statistics issued by the Women's Bureau of the Labor Department, there were 31.4 million women workers by the end of

1969, or about 38.5 percent of the nation's labor force. About 1.6 million women were added to the labor force in 1969, compared with only 700,000 men. The bureau predicted female workers would number 36 million by 1980.

THE LOCKHORNS

"WHY DON'T YOU GO TO BED? YOU CAN HARDLY KEEP YOUR MOUTH OPEN."

© King Features Syndicate, Inc., 1968. World rights reserved.

("I'm in possession of more unemployed friends now than I've ever been in my life, and most of them are male," Barbara Sears, an employee of an educational publishing house, told a *New York Times* reporter recently.)

But most of the male liberators can be found working in the area of divorce-law reform. It is their view that, in the feminist America of the twentieth century, millions of divorced men have become *de facto* slaves to a court system that enables a neurotic wife with a minor complaint to run off with a man's house, his property, his savings, much of his paycheck, and his children, and to jail him if he doesn't cooperate. This is a time when popular books are being written about how to explain divorce to children and teaching couples how to fight. "A fight a day keeps the doctor away," advises one psychologist. "Couples who fight together stay together; . . . a happy marriage is a turbulent marriage."

The male liberators are objecting to an America that encourages its lawyers to earn fortunes separating, divorcing, committing, and recommitting spouses. They are objecting to an America whose greatest writers and novelists have gained their fame as war correspondents on the male-female battlefront.

Raymond L. Perkins, Jr., director of the New England regional district of United States Divorce Reform, Inc., in Essex, Massachusetts, is striving to, as the group's motto declares, "Make America Safe for Marriage." George Doppler, chairman of Pennsylvania's USDR, has been fighting the good fight for many years, and allows that it's tough going and his soul is getting a bit weary. Edward Eddington, who declares that "the minute you hear the judge sentence you to alimony, you join a fraternity of crippled men," founded Alimony Limited in New York.

Frederick L. Clark of Ann Arbor, Michigan, joined the divorce reform movement after noticing a recent vital statistics column in his local newspaper. "I compared them," he says, "thusly: divorce over marriage, 35 to 18; divorce over death, 35 to 5; divorce over birth, 35 to 9; divorce in favor of women, 26 to 9 . . ." He adds, "Judges belong in insane asylums for being men who grant divorces to women the way they wouldn't want a divorce granted to their wives."

Hugh E. Geyer of Morristown, New Jersey, is the vice-president of an international corporation. He is also a provocative and prolific writer, and for several years has submitted articles to various magazines on the subject of what he calls "The Great American Put-Down." Says Geyer: "Look back into history and you will find the inescapable fact that every civilization, no matter how affluent or intelligent, started its last swift *schuss* into national oblivion down the ski slope of matriarchy ... When married men glibly and unhesitatingly refer to their wives as Mama rather than using their given names, it's pretty late in the day for everybody." Geyer has not been able to find anyone to publish his articles.

THE LOCKHORNS

"WELL···· I THINK IF WE COULD OBTAIN A HOME-IMPROVEMENT LOAN, WE COULD SWING A DIVORCE."

Curiously, some of the male liberators are coming from the ranks of lawyers and judges. Says Samuel G. Kling, a divorce lawyer and author of *The Complete Guide to Divorce*: "Women's emancipation is another major reason marriages fail. Before women were emancipated, they settled more or less happily for being wives and mothers. Today the very word 'housewife' is an apology. Emancipation—legal, intellectual, sexual, and financial—has made women much more independent. Now they can walk out and either go to work or get married again. Of course, some women have over-reacted to their newfound freedom. They are shrill, aggressive, and emasculating, becoming the rivals and competitors of their husbands instead of their helpmates. Believing that anything their men do they can do better, such wives have lost their charm, allure, and most precious asset—their femininity."

It should also not go unnoticed that the man who founded the Committee for Fair Divorce and Alimony Laws and led a successful fight to reform New York State's antiquated divorce law was an attorney, Sid Siller of New York. The state's original divorce law, with adultery as the only grounds, was sponsored by Alexander Hamilton, notes Siller. "The problems he left us are considerable when you realize that his own mother and father were not married."

Siller's group is currently pushing for uniform nationwide laws on divorce, alimony, and child custody and for the abolishment of the state's alimony jail. Siller calls most of the states' divorce and alimony laws throwbacks to medieval times when women had no property rights in their own names. "Today in the United States," he says, "women hold over 75 percent of the country's wealth in their own names. We don't want that percentage increased by alimony payments. There is more alimony paid yearly in the U.S. than the cost of the Vietnam conflict . . . We lock a man up if he fails alimony. A felon can have his sentence remitted for good behavior, but not a man in jail for failure to pay alimony."

Still another judge, Stewart A. Newblatt of Michigan, resigned his judgeship recently at the age of forty-two, using words like "unjust, ludicrous, cruel, and barbaric" to describe the state's divorce law. He said, "I can no longer apply an archaic and cruel divorce law that prevents a court from properly performing in the best interests of the parties, the children, and the public. We leave kids with the mother when they ought not to be, because we have glorified the mother."

Another male liberator, William L. Avery, of Franklin, New York, who prefers the term "masculist," sees the feminist movement as the "covert force under the consumption-oriented 'mainstream,' begat by the robber barons after the Civil War." Avery believes that the masculists "are—make no mistake about it—the underground of the future." After he learned of the formation of SEAM, he wrote: "It seems incredible that *The New York Times* even reported on SEAM. I have spent over twenty years of my adult life studying the psychology and the politics of the Feminist-Materialist-Socialist plot to eliminate the middle-class male a la Marx, and am currently trying to get publishers to take a fair-sized volume on the subject. I hope you are as serious as I am on the subject, for time is fast running out.

"Perhaps it is presumptuous of me to intimate that you might not be dead serious about the meaning of your venture. I assure you, from what I have learned in writing my book, that we are the underground of the future—make no mistake about it . . . It is a terrifying picture. From all I read and have read, I tell you that SEAM can become a true revolutionary organization (as your mail must surely indicate). My friends, you have opened Pandora's box. The whole secret of feminism lies in Pandora's box and the sweet approaches to it. We must meet the bitches—male and female —on their own ground."

At last word, Mr. Avery's book remains unpublished.

Not a few male liberators, frustrated in their efforts to win equality for the male, are prepared to call for violence, if necessary, to insure that equality. R. F. Doyle of Long Beach, Mississippi, recently issued a "Manifesto of the Men's Liberation Movement" in which he declared, among other things:

"Women and government agencies have encroached upon male functions, compromised male respect, and relegated many to the status of second-class citizens . . . Women clamor for 'equality' from an already superior position. May whatever gods there be grant this request."

THE LOCKHORNS

"MY IDEA OF A COMPLETE IDIOT
IS A BIGAMIST."

Doyle attacked the "sacred cow syndrome" of the courts which "indiscriminately provides women, regardless of merit, with incentive to divorce . . . Small wonder women initiate 90 percent of divorces." He also attacked the double standard in the courts, wherein the ratio of female convictions to female guilt is far lower than that of male convictions to male guilt. "If a man looks into a home in which a woman is undressing, he will be convicted of window peeping. Reverse the situation with the woman looking in, and he will be convicted of indecent exposure." Doyle notes that "no judge has ever ordered a woman to cook, clean, and sew for her ex-husband."

Doyle also observes that "about 40 percent of the public welfare budgets, and probably the same percentage of correctional institution budgets, are directly attributable to divorce . . . If the proper, natural breadwinner is sabotaged, expenditures for these services to be performed by father-substitute agencies skyrocket, much to the glee of empire-building civil servants therein. Hence their mother-orientation."

Doyle has called for a general strike against alimony. "Perhaps," he says, "by throwing the courts, welfare agencies, and jails into chaos, reform will be demanded. Those who systematically condemn children to live with and fathers to the bondage of unfit mothers, have little interest in morality, the family, or the welfare of children," he declares.

According to Doyle, "reform hasn't been, and apparently will not be, accomplished without coercion or at least civil disobedience. If the reasonable approach to justice fails, the authority of a government so retarded must be defied. It deserves only to be ignored, evaded, or attacked by whatever means and at whatever cost . . . Judicial prejudice that is destroying families and rendering children fatherless is downright criminal stupidity and should be dealt with accordingly. Fire must be fought with fire, and sometimes with dynamite. Guerilla tactics, employed by a dedicated minority, are highly effective . . . The lives of a dozen judges and lawyers would be a more than acceptable trade for the preservation of families and restoration of justice. A society that permits its defenders to return from the wars to helplessly witness the destruction of their families with the outright connivance of local government agencies is perhaps not fit to live in . . . If this be sedition, so be it."

Doyle's manifesto has not, of course, been published.

James W. Wright of Phoenix, Arizona, foresees a new order in America where all women will be required by law to be educated to be wives and mothers first, and will be forced to pass a mandatory examination before male judges. In his new order, Wright proposes that "any woman convicted of back talk and/or castigation of a married man must be shamed publicly by wearing a muzzle and any other appropriate penance . . . A wife who failed to keep house for her spouse would receive the same punishment as a man would receive for failure to provide. Any judge, magistrate, or commissioner showing partiality to women must, on conviction, spend one year in jail and/or be castrated." Incorrigible women, Wright suggests, would face loss of citizenship, exile, or the firing squad.

Fascinating Womanhood

A number of women's organizations have formed recently to support the masculinist view. The Pussycats, whose headquarters are in New York, believe in coddling their men. In Santa Barbara, California, Mrs. Helen B. Andelin, a mother of eight, has organized the Fascinating Womanhood Foundation.

A few years ago Mrs. Andelin wrote a book called *Fascinating Womanhood*. In it she declared that "never before in

history has there been a generation of women so disillu-
sioned, disappointed, and unhappy in marriage as in our
times." So many women, she claimed, are "content with hell,
for they have never known heaven." A woman's most fundamental need, she claimed, is "to be loved and cherished by
her man." And if her man doesn't feel that way about her,
"it's entirely the woman's fault."

Mrs. Andelin observed that "the things that we women
admire in each other are rarely attractive to men," and she
proceeded to draw a portrait of "the ideal woman from a
man's point of view." Mrs. Andelin believes that a woman
should strive to cultivate her femininity and stay out of the
business world. A woman, she claims, can "gain true happiness in marriage" by placing the "husband's happiness as a
primary goal." The Taj Mahal, she notes, was built by the
Indian ruler Shah Jahan in memory of his wife. "Have we
earned such love and devotion from our man?" she asks.

Mrs. Andelin tells us that she sent her manuscript around
to many publishers, but "it seems the major publishers had
some doubts as to the interest women would have in *Fascinating Womanhood*." Undaunted, she formed her own
publishing company. "It has been interesting to us," she says,
"how far the major publishers missed on this, since the book
has already sold nearly 200,000 copies in hardback." The
Andelin organization now plans to sponsor a national
Womanhood Day annually.

In Honolulu, Mrs. Liz Shupe, a mother of four, has formed
a sister organization called Man's Rib. "We do not see man as
the enemy," she says, "but feel sure that we were plucked
from the rib closest to his heart, and that our lives would be
pointless without him."

Not long ago, many of the masculinist organizations held a
national conference in Philadelphia to discuss divorce reform.

There was also talk of merging the groups into a united front to confront their adversaries at all levels.

The most encouraging sign is that many of these groups are now merging to take united action. On April 17, 1971, at Elk Grove, Illinois, the leaders of eighteen divorce-reform organizations met and announced that they had formed the National Council for Family Preservation (NCFP). A momentous and historic meeting, it nonetheless went unreported by the nation's press, which was too busy chasing Germaine Greer and Jane Fonda. Richard F. Doyle was named executive director and an office was opened at 343 S. Dearborn, Suite 1505, in Chicago. Doyle announced that the group's first coordinated activity would be a Father's Day demonstration.

It is encouraging, too, that many black men are rebelling against the matriarchy in which they live. In West Hollywood, Florida, a middle-aged black fugitive from a Georgia chain gang was quoted as saying he felt "saved" when the governor of Georgia informed him that he would not press extradition. But as for Governor Maddox's suggestion that the fugitive return to his wife in Georgia, that was something else. "I don't think I can buy that," he said. "My wife's a repeater. She's been married two or three times. She wants to have her way. The Good Book says a wife should always submit to her husband's will, but my wife, she didn't go for that much. A woman's been married two or three times, she's a little hard to get along with."

"American women," a Greek man recently observed, "yell about their rights when they are with their boyfriends, but when summer comes and their daddies give them some travel money, they run off to vacation in Italy or Greece, where they spend their time chasing around men who take no nonsense from them."

It is also encouraging to see a number of eminent men speak their minds on the subject. In a rare display of courage, Dr. Edgar F. Berman, a heart surgeon and a close personal friend of former Vice-President Hubert H. Humphrey, recently challenged the suitability of women for important jobs, arguing that physical factors, particularly the menstrual cycle and menopause, disqualified women for key executive jobs. The issue came up at a meeting of the Democratic Party's Committee on National Priorities on April 30, 1970, when Representative Patsy T. Mink of Hawaii urged her party to "give the cause of women's rights the highest priority it deserves."

Replied Dr. Berman, a member of the committee: "If you had an investment in a bank, you wouldn't want the president of your bank making a loan under these raging hormonal influences at that particular period. Suppose we had a menopausal woman President in the White House who had to make the decision of the Bay of Pigs, which of course was a bad one, or the Russian contretemps with Cuba at the time?"

He continued: "There are physiologic limitations that women just can't get around, no matter what. There are physical and psychological inhibitants that limit a female's potential. So I reiterate, all things being equal, I would still rather have had a male J.F.K. make the Cuban missile crisis decisions than a female of similar age who could possibly be subject to the curious mental aberrations of that age group. I also say that it would be safer to entrust a male pilot's reactions and judgments in a difficult in-flight or landing problem than to even a slightly pregnant female pilot."

Other Americans are beginning to raise the question of whether male-female separatism might not be a good thing. The U.S. Office of Education recently conducted an experiment in sexually segregated schooling at Jackson Elementary

School in Greeley, Colorado. The experiment was inspired by several studies which had shown that most children with poor school adjustment are boys. Some educators had suggested that boys get off on the wrong foot by starting school with girls. Little boys, they found, tended to develop inferiority feelings, because most often, the teachers were female and tended to favor, reward, and push along the little girls. The boys soon hate to go to school.

In the Greeley experiment, females—both teachers and little girls—were excluded from the school's kindergarten and first grade. Boys exposed to the all-male classes taught by male teachers were different, had better attendance records, were better able to enter discussions, and were better behaved, according to a report in the journal *Nation's Schools*. Curiously, girls do equally well in sexually segregated or coed classes, the report found.

In Miami, not long ago, after an outbreak of vandalism, fistfights, and pranks on his bus, a school-bus driver decided to segregate his bus by sex. He ordered the girls to sit in the back of the bus, and the vandalism and fistfights stopped as soon as the boys and girls were separated. The bus driver's right to segregate the sexes was challenged by the father of one of the girls, but in one of those rare triumphs of patriarchal justice, the Dade County school board upheld the bus driver.*

Samra's Footnote
* The legal aspects of the feminists' drive for equal rights nationally are intriguing. The feminists, in recent years, have gone increasingly to the courts in pursuit of equal rights and equal employment, and the courts, more often than not, have ruled in their favor, particularly as regards discriminatory job practices. On the other hand, the Bill of Rights—that

THE LOCKHORNS

is, the First Amendment—guarantees that "Congress shall make no law respecting an establishment of religion or prohibiting the free exercise thereof." If that is so, then an employer of the Hindu, Buddhist, Jewish, Christian, or Moslem faith, who takes his faith seriously, would be within his rights to refuse to hire a female applicant on the sole religious grounds that a woman's place is in the home. It would make an interesting test case for an employer to challenge before the Supreme Court the sex provision of the Civil Rights Act on grounds that the First Amendment guaranteeing freedom of religion allows one to discriminate on grounds of sex. It is my understanding that a move is afoot at this time to bring just such a test case before the Supreme Court, and some of the historical material in this book will be placed in evidence. I asked a city attorney, whose council had just approved an ordinance prohibiting discrimination by sex, what he would do in the event someone brought a test case on religious grounds. "That's a tough one," he said. "I suppose I'd run."

Samra's Prophecy

It is thus that we come, at last, to Samra's Prophecy, and that is:

Before the end of the twentieth century, a masculinist movement of great proportions will regenerate and revitalize the churches and synagogues of America, or a new masculinist religion will arise, with a new prophet, which will sweep the country and capture the hearts and minds of all nations, bringing them together and their women and children to heel.

In those days, the lion shall lie down with the lamb, women shall hold their tongues, children shall obey their parents, and men shall once more write poetry to women. And peace shall reign forever and ever.

Amen.

Appendix

AT LAST

I am glad to to see the American male is fighting back at last.
> Patricia Coffin, Editor
> Modern Living Department
> *Look*

YOU'VE GOT THE MAKINGS OF A POPULAR ORGANIZATION

I'd like to do a story on your group, angling it for the Father's Day issue of *The Boston Globe*. I'm looking forward to seeing the initial copy of "The American Patriarch." I think you've got the makings of a popular organization.
> Richard W. O'Donnell
> Editorial Department
> *The Boston Globe*

WOMAN EDITOR WANTS TO JOIN LADIES AUXILIARY

As a wife and mother who deserves to be put in her place sometimes, I support what you are trying to do. If you have an auxiliary planned, I'll work on it. Thanks loads.
> Ginny Potter
> Women's Department
> *Morristown Daily Record*
> Morristown, N.J.

Bill Robinson, *The New York Daily News*

AND THAT WAS THAT

To SEAM is to join, says one of Webster's definitions. So it is only appropriate that a new organization aimed at erasing the "matriarchal" society in the United States should call itself SEAM. One of the founders of the Society is Kahlil Samra, 38, married and the father of two infant sons, a former newspaperman and until recently president of and executive director of a national organization doing research in psychiatric problems . . . I asked Samra who's boss in his home. "I am," he said. And that was that.

Gay Pauley
UPI Women's Editor

LET THE LADIES TAKE ON MORE BURDENS

Every rugged, pipe-smoking, tweed-suited man will be cheered by the news from Ann Arbor of the establishment of the Society for the Emancipation of the American Male, a group dedicated to making a man once more the lord and master in the home—and, we dare say, wherever else he may happen to be. Here is a real, red-blooded, no namby-pamby idea . . . Chivalry may be dead, and nobody nowadays may pray the Lord to bless the ladies. But why stop them as they clamor to take on more of the world's burdens, large and small? . . . Sensible men have had experience enough of load-carrying to be perfectly happy to sit down under a shady tree and rest for a while. The real way to male emancipation is the way that leads to the nearest good fishing stream.

Editorial
St. Louis Post-Dispatch

WE'RE NOT BLAMING WOMEN

The founder of the Society for the Emancipation of the American Male believes that patriarchies such as Ireland,

Italy, and Latin America have a lot to teach America. Father rules supreme, and the women are joyful in their feminine roles. . . . "We're not blaming women," he says, "The responsibility is entirely the male's, and he must be the one to correct it."

Mary Caldwell
The Louisville Times

SEAM "SOUNDS GREAT" BUT MAYBE TOO OPTIMISTIC

There is little doubt that American women are rapidly taking over this country, while the men are sitting back and letting them do it. In the home, Dad exists only as a sort of servant-straight man for a nagging wife and her smart-mouthed kids . . . One group is tired of it all—the Society for the Emancipation of the American Male. It hopes to do something to offset the progress the women have made in botching up themselves, their families, and the country. The Society sounds great, although it may be a little optimistic.

Richard O. Pitner
The Birmingham News

"YOU'VE COME A LONG WAY, BABY"

Nobody agrees more with the feminist declaration, "You've come a long way, baby!" than Kahlil Samra, spokesman for the newly organized Society for the Emancipation of the American Male (SEAM). It's just that he believes woman-power has resulted in "botching up themselves, their families, and the country." . . . but SEAM is not anti-woman, Mr. Samra declares. "I am not suggesting that we put veils and long black dresses on American women or keep them out of sight. I am suggesting that the pendulum has swung too far in the other direction in this country. Perhaps we can find a

middle ground between the old ways and the new."
Mary Ann Lauricella
Buffalo Courier Express

ONLY MEN WRITE HEADLINES ON THIS PAPER

We have had many comments on SEAM. The headline writer (only men write headlines on this paper) said that the headline ("You've Gone a Long Way Backward, You Guys") refers to men in general. He thought it was a good headline. I did not, but there's nothing I could do to make him change it. At any rate, it was catchy enough to get a wide readership. I enjoyed reading about SEAM and hope that you'll keep me on your mailing list. I'm most interested and intrigued by SEAM.

Mary Ann Lauricella
Women's Department
Buffalo Courier Express

SANCTITY TO THE FEMALE ROLE

Kahlil Samra, the founder of the Society for the Emancipation of the American Male, feels the family is worth preserving. The feminists, he says, have gone too far, and this is possibly one of the reasons why the family is being torn apart. Samra believes that if there were more father-oriented homes there would be fewer problems with the children raised in them. He says SEAM was established in response to militant feminist groups such as NOW (National Organization for Women) and the Women's Liberation Movement. But, he adds, "We're not militantly anti-feminist. We think there is sanctity to the female role and that it should be treated with a certain amount of respect and gentleness."

Lowell McKirgan
Associated Press

WOMEN DIDN'T INVENT EVIL

The Society for the Emancipation of the American Male believes the United States is a matriarchy, and they want to make it a patriarchy . . . The idea that women are the root of evil is an ancient cliché which men are happy to honor by way of excusing their own weaknesses. Women surely are capable of participating in evil. We have our Bonnies as well as our Clydes. But women didn't invent evil . . . I think women are a very interesting sex. They are tough and amusing and helpful. I don't think they should wear trousers, though. I like to look at their legs."

Jack Smith
The Los Angeles Times

GETTING AWAY FROM THE BOOB IMAGE

A lot of Greater Boston dads may have received a Father's Day gift this week that they weren't expecting. In Ann Arbor, Mich., the Society for the Emancipation of the American Male has been formed. Its founder declares: "Surely it is no coincidence that psychiatry has prospered and grown alongside the feminist movement in the United States . . . It's time we got away from the television, comic-strip boob image of the American male who exists only as a sort of a servant-straight-man for a nagging wife and her smart-mouth kids." That's the good news this Father's Day. Help is on the way!

Richard W. O'Donnell
The Boston Globe

NEO-FEMINIST MOVEMENT HONORED BY AN AVOWED FOE

The neo-feminist movement, which has more trouble fighting apathy than anything else, has just been honored by an avowed foe—the Society for the Emancipation of the American Male has been organized in Ann Arbor, Mich. It hopes to restore the American male to his rightful place at the head of the family. SEAM plans to publish a quarterly newsletter, "The American Patriarch." Yearly dues are $5 for members of either sex. "Originally we were going to charge $2.50 for our ladies' auxiliary," Mr. Samra said, "but we were afraid so many guys would say, "Why should I pay $5 when my wife can send in $2.50?"

Marylin Bender
The New York Times

DEAR ABIE

The founder's issue of "The American Patriarch," newsletter of the Society for the Emancipation of the American Male, contains an advice-to-the-lovelorn column (called "Dear Abie") offering counsel like: "Woman who treat husband like servant during day cannot expect him to behave like king in bed at night."

Judy Nicol
Chicago Sun-Times News

EMANCIPATION DAY

A Society for the Emancipation of the American Male has been formed. I learned this from a news release that somehow found its way to my desk. Believing my wife should be fully informed of world happenings, I took SEAM's message home. It's the first time I've had Spam for dinner since I left the Army. Not easily intimidated, I pressed on with SEAM's message. SEAM says, "The Holy Scriptures of all nations elevated the male while esteeming the woman who is humble, obedient, and solicitous of her husband," I reported. That's when she poured gravy on my dessert, and the dog headed instinctively for the closet. "Okay, that does it," I growled. "Do you know know what else SEAM says? SEAM says, "It's time we got away from the teevee, comic-strip boob image of the American male who exists only as a sort of servant-straight-man for a nagging wife and her smart-mouth kids." "You're too old to change now," she offered, pushing the dog and me out the door. "The Hindu sage, Vatsyayana, once said, 'A virtuous woman, who has affection for her husband, should act in conformity with his wishes as if he were a divine being," I yelled back through the keyhole. A distant voice within the house floated back: "Give him a good walk or you'll have to clean up the mess."

Al Blanchard
The Detroit News

RALLY 'ROUND THE FLAG, BOYS!

Rally 'round the flag boys! A new banner has just been unfurled. It heralds the formation of the Society for the Emancipation of the American Male, an organization dedicated to "restoring the American patriarchy" and returning the male to "his rightful place at the head of the family."

Doris Blake
The New York Daily News

MALE POWER

The trouble with this country is that it isn't being run by men any more. This country is being run by women; it is being run by kids; it is being run, in part, by some men who might as well be women or kids. The time has now come for all good men to do something about this deplorable mess. One good man is doing something about it. He is Kahlil

Samra, of Ann Arbor, Mich., who last April, organized the Society for the Emancipation of the American Male. Kahlil Samra has compiled some staggering statistics to prove his point . . . The important thing that Kahlil Samra is trying to do is simply to convince American males to assert their manhood by demanding the return of their rightful authority as head of the family. He believes it is a divine right, evident in the writings and sermons of the founders of all religions. He also points out that personages like Moses, Isaiah, Jesus Christ, Paul the Apostle, Buddha, Mohammed, and Martin Luther—men who were voluble on the women's obedient role in life—all appeared in history to speak at a time when women were getting out of hand, and he believes each appearance was providential . . . Samra maintains: "Whoever originated the idea that marriage is a partnership was either a henpecked husband or a bachelor. No ship can have two captains." Samra says: "The American male has been placed in a position where he must continually try to prove his masculinity . . . At the same time, he is so insecure about his masculinity that he is terrified of developing an affectionate relationship with another man because he fears it might turn queer. So where do we go from here?" Samra feels the only place we can go is back to a patriarchal society. He is confident that once the total manhood-power of the country is united in the crusade for the restoration of the American patriarchy, victory is inevitable. So, men, our course is clear. Let us join behind our leader with this toast: "Kahlil Samra, may your tribe increase!" And don't forget to send your five bucks.

Glenn D. Kittler
Coronet

WOULDN'T YOU KNOW HE'D BE A LEBANESE?

To prove the legend that Lebanese men are attractive to women, especially American women, "because they assert themselves as men" (they won't even carry a package for a woman on the street!) is the following story that appeared recently . . . The Society for the Emancipation of the American Male has been organized in Ann Arbor, Mich., by Kahlil Samra, a former psychiatric research foundation executive who believes that the whole range of psychiatric problems from alcoholism to juvenile delinquency is less prevalent in patriarchies such as Italy, Greece, Japan, and India, where men still rule their homes.

The Lebanese-American Journal

THE THREAD THAT HOLDS SEAM TOGETHER MAY BE A WOMAN

(One day Dennis Chase, a reporter for *The Ann Arbor News*, telephoned the author to ask if he would permit his wife to be interviewed by the paper's women's editor.

"Just a minute," the author said, "and I'll ask her."

The next day, the Associated Press carried a story reporting that the founder of the Society for the Emancipation of the American Male had committed a colossal boo-boo.

Moral: Be careful what you tell the press.

The following are excerpts from Kathie Blackmer's interview with Kathleen Samra:)

The thread that holds SEAM together may just be a woman. She's Mrs. Kahlil M. Samra, wife of SEAM's founder, and a staunch supporter of the organization and her husband. The apparent contradiction of a woman supporting a male emancipation movement dissolves when you meet Kathleen Samra. "I support SEAM heartily—I think what my husband is trying to do is important. We see it the same way . . . A woman should try to support her husband in every way that she can. She should serve him, but not in the slave sense of the word. It's the wife's job to see that his home is peaceful—a place that he wants to come home to." Warm and personable, the wife of SEAM's founder is an attractive young mother who never had any great career plans. "My husband and I basically agree that a woman's place is in the home," she says. "Women seem to approve of the basic idea of holding the family unit together." In a country where there are eight million fathers who have deserted their families, a half-million divorces every year (with one in four marriages ending in divorce), and nine million widows, SEAM's philosophy is food for family thought.

Kathie Blackmer
Women's Editor
The Ann Arbor News

A Few Choice Letters to SEAM from Men

PROFESSOR URGES MALES TO QUESTION THEIR
"HARMFUL HERITAGE"

I could not commend more your efforts to stop the emasculation of the American male. Unfortunately, I fear that this process has gone so far that most young males while dating—i.e., before marriage—accept without asking or thinking as part of our American egalitarian heritage feminism, or the view that a woman is a man except for her appearance. You must get young men to question this harmful heritage.

I felt somewhat like a manic-depressive upon reading your Founding Members issue of *The American Patriarch*. I was elated over the points made on each page, for they are points

Jim Berry
Newspaper Enterprise Association

that must be made and publicized, but upon reaching your stamp on the last page about the temporary discontinuance of the newsletter, I felt a black cloud suddenly suffuse me as when one loses a good friend.

The patriarchal point of view must be publicized regularly, if only to offset the campaigns of the feminists. A patriarchal organization and publication are desperately needed in North America. Hence, *The American Patriarch* MUST be revived.

Why not try sending notices to each of the 2,000-plus colleges and universities, stating succinctly your aims and inviting subscriptions to your newsletter? There are enough male (and female) students who are conscious of and therefore fully opposed to the mass emasculation current in North America and who are just waiting—perhaps unwittingly—for your organization and publication to come along.

Further, there are numberless male students who have been brainwashed into emasculation long before marriage, whose eyes would be opened for the first time to the slavery they have entered unwittingly. You should also send speakers to campuses. Any patriarchally minded speaker will receive a big audience from non-college folk and college students if only because the coeds will show up in droves and the males will come and discuss the provocative lecture with the coeds afterwards—for days probably.

Professor
East Coast University

HAVOC WREAKED UPON BOYS BY FEMALE TEACHERS

I am a high school teacher here in Los Angeles and during the summers I work for a local YMCA counselor. In my continued and close contact with children of this city, mostly boys, I am increasingly aware of the havoc and destruction wreaked upon them by our female-oriented society. Their mothers control their home life, their teachers until at least junior high school are nearly exclusively women, their Sunday-school teachers are female, and they are thrust into the most demanding boy-girl relationships literally before puberty.

THE LOCKHORNS

"I'M SORRY, MR. LOCKHORN. YOU JUST CANNOT WRITE OFF EXPENSES INCURRED BY YOUR WIFE AT THE BEAUTY PARLOR AS A TOTAL LOSS!"

As a result, many of our country's boys (early teens and younger) are looking—and vainly searching—for an acceptable male image on which to pattern their young lives. They can certainly not turn to advertising—if they did, they would have to align themselves with "Virginia Slims" and would be eternally frustrated by not knowing *what* to do with a silly-looking Tampax. They cannot turn to their teachers—what school employee does not live in dread of the "irate mother" while never having heard of the father? They cannot turn to their community leaders—most of them are still fighting the repeal of prohibition along with the suffragettes.

I am intensely interested in this subject, to the point that I am planning the pursuit of a doctorate in psychology. The projected title of my dissertation is "Down With Mama's Boy." Also, I am available for any help I can give your organization. Much good luck in the future.

Gerald Jones
Los Angeles, California

A BACHELOR TALKS ABOUT THE FEMALE 'VULTURES' HE WORKS WITH IN THE FEDERAL GOVERNMENT

Being a bachelor and completely unqualified to join with you, I would still like to express myself regarding this matriarchal mess that exists in this country.

Without question, the biggest employer in the world, the U.S. federal government, is setting the worst example. I am about to retire from federal employment. Through the years I have worked with armies of married women and most of them just didn't need their jobs at all. They should have been home behind the kitchen sink as far as I was concerned. I refer specifically to the ones with husbands in the $15,000-a-year and above class (as of today) in and out of the federal government. How sickening it is to see them come to work in their fine cars, leaving their lovely homes and children (in many cases), to spend the day in a government office where they don't belong. What a bunch of misfits! Frankly, however, I feel this whole mess is a total lost cause, as the practice is so completely entrenched in the lives of so many of these vultures. It would take nothing short of a massive tax revolution to bring about changes. There is all kinds of talk of the evils of Communism (which I don't feel is a direct threat to this country), and yet what do we have destroying us in Washington? The big spenders there will bury us eventually.

For myself, I have a great deal of respect and admiration for women. I am by no means a woman hater. I work with a lot of fine females and some are working because of circumstances in their marriage and they really need their jobs, but there is one heck of a bunch of them on the taxpayers' rolls who are just plain pigs. There seems to be a strong feeling building up against these people who seem to feel they are protected by the phony equal-opportunity-in-employment feature which some clowns in Washington dreamed up (no discrimination because of sex, color, etc.). As it stands now, a person who really needs a job, whether white or colored, would be just plain out of luck as far as federal employment goes, because there are so many good-paying jobs filled by these undeserving females.

I can't help feeling that a change will occur, however. This situation is even being mentioned from the pulpits throughout the country, which is encouraging.

In the federal office where I work we have the biggest collection of money-hungry females you can imagine, many of whom have husbands, etc., and yet the personnel people who do the hiring never ask the women what their husbands do. Many of these have cleaning women to do the chores at home, some send their children to private schools, etc. No wonder so many of us are bitter and disgusted. I personally know that some of these women have husbands who don't want their wives to work, but the women insist on it and get their own way. They want what their husbands get and what they can make, too. . . . Behind the scenes of all this are the totally uninformed taxpayers, the world's biggest bunch of suckers. If they only knew how they were being taken. If more publicity were given to this situation which exists within the federal government, we really would have a tax revolution, which I feel is the only solution to our top-heavy bureaucratic system, anyway. Maybe later on the Nixon administration will come up with some solutions. Let's hope so.

Good luck with your program.

Male Federal Employee

SHE SAID I HAD NO RIGHTS

Perhaps your organization is the answer and the only way to right the wrongs of the present-day, unjust discriminatory practices set against the male. Never did I believe until now how corrupt and obsolete the laws regarding family court are. How they discriminate endlessly in all ways against the male!

To the family court judges, doctors, and attorneys, the human beings involved in these unfortunate matrimonial difficulties are of no importance. The only thing that matters is the amount of money to be made from the case.

To organize is the only way to be heard and recognized.

My wife, like many young girls today, couldn't wait to get married. After five years she got tired and bored of married life. As she described it, she "wants to live now, not later." I worked like a dog for my wife and children, but all she had wasn't enough. She walked out on me. Before leaving, she expressed that I had no rights. I soon found out how true this was.

I believe that if the laws were changed to render equal and fair justice, both male and female would think twice before jumping into divorce. As the laws are now, the woman knows that she has superior rights. She automatically gets custody of the children, usually gets more than sufficient alimony and all kinds of fringe benefits. This is why many young girls today enter into marriage with the attitude that if the marriage doesn't work, so what? I'll get a divorce, alimony, custody and live like a queen.

I am just an average working man. I was a good husband, hard worker, and good provider, loved my wife and children, yet this wasn't enough for my wife. She only thought of herself, not of me or the children.

Each time that I have been to court, I have been threatened either with commitment or with jail.

Deserted Husband
New City, New York

THE LOCKHORNS

"IS THERE ANY WAY YOU CAN SYNCHRONIZE HER MOUTH WITH HER BRAIN?"

ANOTHER GOOD CHRISTIAN MAN BEWITCHED

I am a chemical engineer, married 30 years with five children, whose wife left my home six months ago and has now filed for divorce. I have no vices except possibly smoking a cigar occasionally. I have an excellent reputation as an engineer and am respected everywhere except in the home.

I might add that during the last 14 years, my wife and I have developed a business which she manages in which I put a considerable amount of money and all my spare time. The business floundered for 13 years. Now that the business has pointed upward, the wife has been planning to ease me out in a series of secret moves—assuming an indicia of ownership, adding riders to the longtime business insurance in her favor, changing or eliminating me as beneficiary in a total of $50,000 of life insurance, diverting funds to numerous accounts, withholding business records, and finally, when I asked for an accounting, she pulls out. In doing so, she "buys" the five children with money made from the business I financed and helped to build.

Also in doing this she wrecked my chances for promotion and salary increases. She left a longtime membership at the Episcopal Church, and is now attending a "group" meeting where they discuss problems of psychology.

We have extensive real estate holdings. It was like dropping an atom bomb. She told me she was going to take me for everything I have. I have never been untrue and have had too much patience and trust. I let her handle ALL finances for 29 years. I have never been in court before in my life. I simply don't understand why the courts will even consider a case such as hers.

As it stands now, I, a respectable father, citizen, Christian, find myself abandoned by the wife and five children, having all left the day after Christmas, and sued for divorce by a lawyer touted to be a "divorce expert." I don't see how he can find honest reasons for divorce.

The business now nets 50 percent more than I make as an engineer. I have never participated in any profits, yet I have been tapped for $50 per week for my daughter, and she is trying for alimony, temporary and permanent, and asking me to pay all court costs.

This is unfair. I was planning to retire in another year, and now I find myself in position of being stripped. I have already spent considerable amounts of money in legal fees and defense.

Also, my health has been affected somewhat. The mental strain imposed by her mad-dog action is bound to take its toll . . . I am in court now and need any help you might be in a position to give me to prevent me from being stripped.

Good Christian Man

THE GIRLS ARE GETTING THE MAXIMUM WHILE GIVING THE MINIMUM

Words can't express how happy I was to learn of the formation of SEAM. Do we dare to dream it might just be possible to put a dent in the haughty arrogance of the typical American female who has been used to getting the maximum while giving the minimum?

Kindly mail me (in a *plain* envelope—landlady!) the Society's newsletter. May God bless you and your work.

Bachelor
Harrisburg, Pennsylvania

ADULTERESS AWARDED CUSTODY OF HIS CHILDREN

I was very much impressed by Glenn Kittler's article in the November issue of *Coronet*. There was so much truth expertly expressed which I have never seen written before, but there was one important thing left out. I believe most henpecked men are living under constant threat of losing their family or perhaps just their children. They know the courts will give all they have to their wife anytime she is ready to leave him. She doesn't have to let him be "head of the family" and there is nothing he can do about it. He either submits to her every whim or she will make him wish he had. This is why so many men waste their life drinking and are so desperately trying to prove their manhood in every way possible to everyone they meet.

I have been down the hard, rough road of losing my place as head of the family. I feel that I could have handled any and all marital situations until my wife found out what all she could do and still find favor with our legal system. She was right, she could go to almost any extreme and still get custody of my children. She had an illegitimate baby last summer, and even though I was awarded the divorce on the grounds of adultery (the only Scriptural grounds), she was awarded custody of my two children.

No one can realize or imagine a situation such as mine. We all think of the judicial system as being fair until we are caught up in such a situation. No one can imagine me not getting custody of my children unless I gave them just cause. I gave them no cause and there was absolutely no excuse for the legal system to break up my home. They have divided so many homes just by being the way they are. Sometimes it seems more homes are divided than not—just because a man cannot assume his rightful place as "head of the family"!

I got 1,000 copies made of your newsletter to distribute with requests for support and encouragement. I can only say that I feel that you are doing more for all of mankind than anyone else ever has by pursuing this mission of putting the man back at his God-given place as head of the family.

Divorced Husband

AMERICAN FEMALES BOGGLE HIS TEUTONIC MIND

Enclosed please find $10 to pay for your newsletter. I'd

like you to send it to my native Germany. I am soon leaving this beautiful country in order to spare my sons from the brutal brainwash of America's power-hungry and egotistik [sic] females.

> German Male
> New York (en route to Germany)

WHAT IS GOING ON HERE IS TOO MUCH

I read about you in *Coronet* and your idea to unite American men. They are in trouble. We men who come from Europe here we are in some trouble with our women.

I went around Europe see many countries and lot of women, but what is going on here is too much. I am married eight years, have one kid (son). Two time near marriage break but so far I am Bos in my house, how long I don't know. Here I send you money order of $5 for membership. Please let me know is everything O.K.

> Ivan Jagnjic
> Croatian Immigrant
> Bronx, New York

A Last Word from the Ladies

MESSAGE FROM THE WIFE OF A LUCKY MAN—

"EVEN IN CHURCH, THE WOMEN WANT TO RULE THE MEN"

May I join your organization? Your group is the answer to my way of thinking and the only ally I have had or read about in my nineteen years of marriage.

My husband is definitely the head of this home and will remain so.

I believe in women living on what the husband makes and in women staying home.

Give America back to the men and give the mothers back to the children. Take married women off the payrolls and put the unemployed men on; make more jobs available for the children coming out of high school.

I am tired of women talking down their husbands and I am sick of seeing children running wild while mothers work and belong to clubs.

If I join your organization, it will be the only one I belong to and I have only one reason for joining yours.

My main reason is the support that I will have in teaching my attitudes to my three daughters. Church helps a great deal, but even in church the women want to rule the men, and our country has dwindled from a strong male-dominated land to a land that has no set of values on anything.

Men are the greatest and they built a great world. Since woman has been taking over, it seems to have gone downhill.

Material things cannot be kept intact for very long, but a well-reared child and a happy husband can have an influence on the world that can last forever.

Men are the happiest when they are running the ship, and whether they run it right or wrong at all times is unimportant, just as long as they are happy and can have the self-respect to get it going right after a little wrong.

Women think they are doing so great, but when they get in a little pinch it is always a man that gets them out. If women keep downgrading men, we are not going to have any help, then where will women be?—blaming the men, poor guys.

I am thirty-eight and have three daughters—fifteen, twelve, and seven. My daughter tells me I am a nobody because I don't work or belong to anything outside the home. I tell my daughter I am a somebody because I have the stamina to stay home and do for only my husband and children, and I need no accolades from the world to fulfill my birthright. Doing what I feel is correct takes more will power today than at any other time in history and believe me, I, and other women who feel as I do, need your organization more than your group needs us.

Happy Housewife

THE LOCKHORNS

"THE ONLY MAN I KNOW WHO USES THE REMOTE CONTROL TO TURN ON THE EXERCISE PROGRAM."

CONFOUNDED BY THE "TAME" AMERICAN MALE

Three hearty cheers for SEAM! As a female (British), I endorse anything you can do to promote masculine sovereignty in the home. I am perpetually appalled by the role (or rather, non-role) played by the average domesticated (tame?) American male. Frankly, I've never really understood how they could maintain their subordination without blowing their stacks more often; when they do, it is usually detrimentally.

I don't think that there is any woman who, if she were to be 100% honest, would not agree that she would prefer to be gently but firmly dominated by a man. One has only to look at most women's ordinary, everyday expressions and attitudes to realize that they are not at peace with themselves or anyone else, including their own children . . . I am convinced, and have been for some time, that a great part of this country's social problems is based on the vast number of individually unsatisfactory sexual relationships, both in and out of bed.

I wish you every success in your venture and look forward to hearing more about it.

British Female
Ann Arbor, Michigan

IT'S FOR SURE NO ONE WILL FORGET YOU

Yes, surely the Bible tells us that we women were made for men and men for God. My father was the patriarch in our home and my husband is in ours.

The fact that there are many possibilities for humor in connection with SEAM may prove of great help. With all the laughter and jokes there were about the women lynching you after your address at the Order of St. Luke conference in Philadelphia, it is for sure that no one will forget you, and I'm afraid that could not be said of all the speakers.

Mrs. Jack Stewart
Scottsdale, Arizona

START WITH YOUNG PEOPLE—THE OTHERS ARE TOO FAR GONE

I am twenty-two and a bride of eleven months. May I congratulate you? Not too long ago I heard someone say that "the wife is head of the house *BUT* the husband is head of the home." Beautiful, don't you think? I wish you much success in what you are trying to do. I feel, though, that it could only begin with my generation . . . the others are too far gone. Good luck.

Mrs. Karyn R. Wilson
Bell Gardens, California

Masculinist and Law-Reform Organizations

The Society for the Preservation
of Early American Standards
R. J. Fahey, Chairman
RD No. 2
Oxford, N.Y.

Lloyd F. Murphy (in formation)
Lloyd F. Murphy & Associates, Inc.
730 Chicago Ave.
Minneapolis, Minn. 55415

Fund for the Preservation of
the Family
Lillian S. Busby
2065 N. Rodney Dr.
Los Angeles, Calif. 90027

National Council for Family
Preservation
Richard F. Doyle, Executive
Director
343 S. Dearborn
Suite 1505
Chicago, Ill. 60604

The Pussycats
(a group of women who believe
in coddling their men)
Jeannie Sakol, President
230 E. 48th St.
New York, N.Y.

Committee for Fair Divorce &
Alimony Laws
Sid Siller, Founder
509 Fifth Ave.
New York, N.Y. 10017

United States Divorce
Reform, Inc.
National Headquarters,
George Partis, Director
P. O. Box 243
Kenwood (Valley of the Moon),
Calif.

Anti-Divorce Rackets Group
P. O. Box 1809
Seattle, Wash.

National Churchmen for
Legal Reform, Inc.
Rev. Philip M. Lenud, President
1970 Glynn Court
Detroit, Mich.

Wisconsin Institute on
Divorce, Inc.
M. Ianelli
P. O. Box 1905
Milwaukee, Wis. 53201

U.S. Divorce Reform, Inc.
New England Regional Office
Raymond L. Perkins, Director
P. O. Box 253
Essex, Mass. 01929

Masculinist and Law-Reform Organizations

U.S. Divorce Reform, Inc.
Central East Coast Office
George F. Doppler, Director
P. O. Box 60
Broomall, Pa. 19008

USDR
130 Newton St.
Hartford, Conn. 06105

USDR
1115 Laurel Ave.
Ypsilanti, Mich. 48197

USDR
1409 Camden Dr.
Charleston, W. Va. 25301

Missouri Council on
   Family Law
Gene Austin
608 Kingsland Ave.
St. Louis, Mo. 63120

American Society of Divorced Men
486 Mary Place
Elgin, Ill. 60120

Layman's Grievance League
Edwin T. Jagiello
Box 1
New York Mills, N.Y. 13417

Chicago Divorce Court Victims
   Club
1679 Webster Lane
Desplaines, Ill.

Committee to Reform
   California's Judicial System
P. O. Box 245
San Pablo, Calif.

In Pro-Per, Inc.
John H. Adair
P. O. Box 3374
Huntington Park, Calif. 90255

Juvenile Rights Foundation
Box 645
Beverly Hills, Calif.

Committee to Clean Up the Courts
Sherman Skolnick, Chairman
9800 S. Oglesby Ave.
Chicago, Ill. 60617

Marital Health Publishing Co.
James Waller
P. O. Box 20861
Atlanta, Ga. 30320

Defense Against Women's
   Maintenance & Alimony
M. Revelman
P. O. Box 76
Brighton, Vic. 3186,
   Australia

Masculinist and Law-Reform Organizations

Catholic Society of Divorced Men
Stanley V. Tucker
130 Newton St.
Hartford, Conn. 06105

Nebraska Council on Family Law
920 N. 68th St.
Lincoln, Nebr.

Judean Society (Divorced
Catholic Women)
Frances Miller
756 Lois Ave.
Sunnyvale, Calif. 94087

Divorced Men's Club
2012 Washington
Albuquerque, N. M.

U.S. Anti-Shyster League
96 Otis St.
Bangor, Maine 04401

Family Education & Information
Council of the U.S.
(Publishers of U.S. Basic
Unit News)
M. Ann Evans
P. O. Box 386
Corona Del Mar, Calif. 92625

Marriage Insurance Institute
P. O. Box 9874
Philadelphia, Pa. 19140

Society for the Emancipation
of the American Male
P. O. Box 211
Ann Arbor, Mich. 48107

Divorce Law Reform Union
39 Clabon News
London S.W., England

Family Counseling Centers, Inc.
49 Franklin St.
Boston, Mass. 02215

Layman's Law League
8536 S. Peoria St.
Chicago, Ill. 60620

Court Victim's Association
129 S. Monterey St.
Alhambra, Calif. 91801

Alimony, Inc.
New York City

American Divorce Reform Laws
P. O. Box 282
Cuyahoga Falls, Ohio

American Fair Trial Association
9404 Flower Ave.
Silver Spring, Md. 20901

Divorced Catholic Men
14419 Brink Ave.
Norwalk, Calif. 90650

Masculinist and Law-Reform Organizations

Freedom, Inc.
P. O. Box 2510
Texarkana, Tex. 75501

Marriage & Divorce Law
  Reform League
8940 Lauder
Detroit, Mich.

Fascinating Womanhood
P. O. Box 3617
Santa Barbara, Calif. 93105

Man's Rib
Honolulu, Hawaii

Committee for Common Sense
  Divorce Laws
John W. Biggert
1875 DuPont Ave.
Memphis, Tenn. 38127

Lawyer Reform of the
  United States
1480 W. Bayshore Rd.
Palo Alto, Calif. 94303

Fathers United for Equal Rights
Box 9751
Baltimore, Md. 21204

Society of Second Wives
2 East Lake St.
Minneapolis, Minn. 55408

(The following "Declaration of Dependence" was circulated recently by the Fascinating Womanhood Movement of Santa Barbara, California.)

𝔇𝔢𝔠𝔩𝔞𝔯𝔞𝔱𝔦𝔬𝔫 𝔬𝔣 𝔇𝔢𝔭𝔢𝔫𝔡𝔢𝔫𝔠𝔢

We, the undersigned, accept the following concepts as basic to the best interest and welfare of women, their families and the nation:

1. We believe that the man should be the breadwinner and head of the family.

2. We believe that women should be feminine and dependent, devoting themselves to the feminine arts and creating happy homes.

3. We believe that the greatest contribution that a woman can make to the well being of society is in the home, successfully fulfilling her role as a wife, mother and homemaker.

4. We recognize that women have talents and time to give outside the home, but believe that they should be secondary to her greater responsibility in the home.

5. We believe that men and women are different physically, psychologically, tempermentally, and socially and therefore are not created to be equals in responsibility.

6. We believe that a greater state of happiness exists for both men and women when men are masculine, dominant and aggressive, assuming their responsibility to guide, protect and provide for the family, and when women are feminine, trustful and dependent, devoting themselves to their feminine role. We do not believe in equating the sexes.

7. We oppose free child care centers. They will encourage women to neglect the home.

8. We oppose legalized abortion on request. Our bodies may be our own, but the unborn child is not our own. It is an individual due rightful protection of the law. It cannot protect itself.

9. We oppose any amendment to the Constitution which will provide equality of the sexes, if at the same time it removes protective labor laws, protective marriage laws, etc., and causes women to become subject to the draft.

THE STRENGTH OF AMERICA LIES IN THE HOME